Letters *from the* Battlefront

The Vietnam War

VIRGINIA SCHOMP

NEW YORK

In memory of Jeffrey T. Schomp (1946–1971)
and for all the men and women who made it home,
and those who never will

Benchmark Books
Marshall Cavendish
99 White Plains Road
Tarrytown, New York 10591-9001
www.marshallcavendish.com

Text copyright © 2004 by Marshall Cavendish Corporation
Map © 2004 by Marshall Cavendish Corporation
Map by Laszlo Kubinyi

Library of Congress Cataloging-in-Publication Data

Schomp, Virginia.
The Vietnam War / by Virginia Schomp.
p. cm. — (Letters from the battlefront)
Summary: Describes the Vietnam Conflict through the letters of the
people who fought it, including war supporters and objectors, African
Americans and Hispanics, pilots, soldiers, and combat nurses.
Includes bibliographical references and index.
ISBN 0-7614-1663-3
1. Vietnamese Conflict, 1961-1975—Personal narratives,
American—Juvenile literature. [1. Vietnamese Conflict,
1961-1975—Personal narratives.] I. Title II. Series: Schomp,
Virginia.   Letters from the battlefront.

DS559.5.S36 2003
959.704'3'0922—dc21   2003009857

Book design by Patrice Sheridan
Art Research: Rose Corbett Gordon & Alexandra H. C. Gordon, Mystic, CT
Cover: Topham/The Image Works
Bettmann/Corbis: pages 7, 11, 20, 22, 35, 61 & 74; Associated Press, AP: pages 15, 37, 52; Topham/The Image Works: pages 17 & 70; Tim Page/Corbis: pages 25, 31 & 54; Mark Godfrey/The Image Works: pages 27 & 65; Jack Novak/SuperStock: page 40; Index Stock/Everett Johnson: page 44; Jonathan Rawle/Stock,Boston: page 46; Hulton Archive/Getty Images: pages 57 & 72; Owen Franken/Stock, Boston: page 68; Tom Miner/The Image Works: page 71.

Printed in China
1 3 5 6 4 2

Contents

From the Author

Letters from the Battlefront is written as a companion to the *Letters from the Homefront* series. The books in that series told the story of America's wars from the viewpoint of those who worked, watched, and waited at home. These books look at the same conflicts through the eyes of the men and women on the front lines.

Historians often study letters and journals written by famous people—explorers, philosophers, kings—to gain information about the past. Recently they have discovered the value of writings by "ordinary" people, too. Students of history have begun to seek out and study the personal writings of farmers and merchants, slaves and slaveholders, sailors and foot soldiers. Documents such as these, often called primary sources, help us to understand the beliefs, hopes, and dreams of earlier generations and to learn how historical events shaped their lives.

This book uses primary sources to recapture the drama of life during the Vietnam War. In these pages you will meet the pilots who fought the air war over Vietnam and the ground troops who faced the dangers of guerrilla combat. You will read the stories of African-American and Hispanic soldiers who struggled against racism in their own ranks. You will hear from the courageous women who nursed the wounded in combat zones. Their letters, journals, and remembrances introduce us to a generation of young Americans struggling to make sense of their ordeals in a confusing, unpopular war far from home.

Tracing the Roots

The roots of American involvement in Vietnam reach back into World War II. During that conflict, Japan occupied French Indochina, the French colony that included Vietnam, Laos, and Cambodia. Ho Chi Minh (hoe-chee-MIN) led the resistance against Japan. A Vietnamese nationalist and Communist, Ho organized a guerrilla army dedicated to the struggle for independence. U.S. government intelligence agents helped supply and train Ho's soldiers and, in return, they reported Japanese troop movements and rescued downed American pilots. At the war's end U.S. agents stood at Ho Chi Minh's side as he announced his country's independence. The opening lines of his statement came from the American Declaration of Independence: "We hold the truth that all men are created equal, that they are endowed by their Creator with certain unalienable rights, among them life, liberty, and the pursuit of happiness."

Ho Chi Minh hoped that his American allies would support his efforts to keep France from regaining control of Vietnam. But U.S. leaders had other concerns. No sooner had World War II ended than a "Cold War" between the forces of democracy and Communism began. Long years of fighting had devastated the democratic nations of Western Europe, leaving the Soviet Union the dominant power in Europe and Asia. The Soviets had already overrun most of Eastern Europe, and now they seemed determined to spread Communism around the globe. To counter that threat, America needed strong

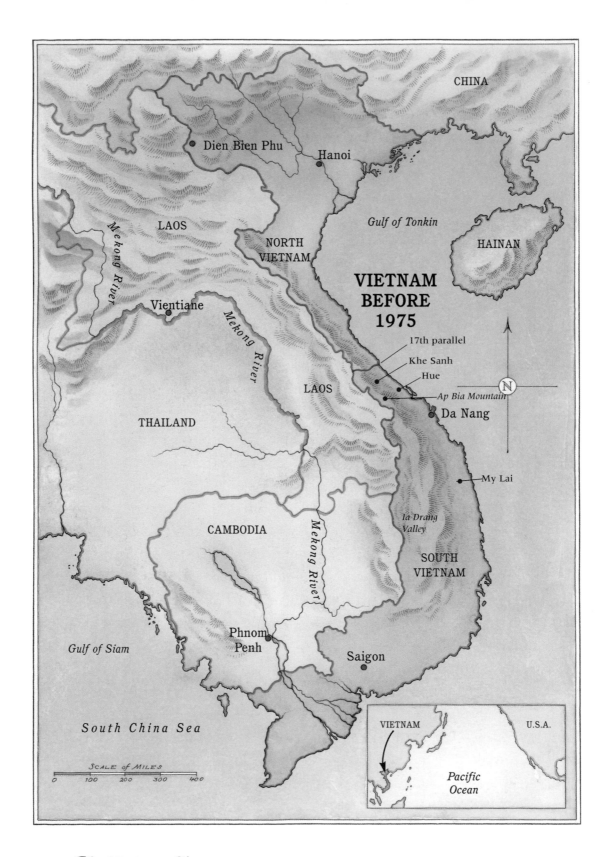

CHINA

Dien Bien Phu

Hanoi

LAOS

NORTH
VIETNAM

Gulf of Tonkin

HAINAN

**VIETNAM
BEFORE
1975**

Mekong River

Vientiane

Mekong River

17th parallel

Khe Sanh

Hue

Ap Bia Mountain

LAOS

Da Nang

THAILAND

My Lai

*Ia Drang
Valley*

CAMBODIA

Mekong River

SOUTH
VIETNAM

Phnom
Penh

Saigon

Gulf of Siam

South China Sea

SCALE of MILES

0   100   200   300   400

VIETNAM

U.S.A.

*Pacific
Ocean*

Vietnamese Communist leader Ho Chi Minh waged guerrilla wars against France and the United States.

European allies. Consequently, when war broke out between France and Vietnam in 1946, President Harry S. Truman ignored Ho's pleas for help. Publicly declaring the United States neutral, Truman secretly provided economic and military aid to France.

Even with U.S. backing, the French were fighting a losing battle in Vietnam. While they gained control of the cities, Ho's fiercely determined fighters held the countryside. The guerrillas waged a war of ambushes, assassinations, and hit-and-run raids that kept the enemy constantly on the defensive. More than 75,000 French soldiers would be killed in what the people of France called *la sale guerre*, "the dirty war."

Meanwhile, the Cold War was heating up. The Soviets tested their first atomic bomb in 1949. That same year a Communist government seized power in China. From 1950 to 1953 the United States fought the Korean War, defending South Korea against an invasion by Communist North Korea. U.S. leaders began to see Vietnam as a centerpiece in the struggle against global Communism. If Vietnam fell to the Communists, they argued, the other nations of Southeast Asia would soon follow. Such a disastrous loss could tip the balance of power against Western Europe and the United States.

Responding to this threat, President Truman abandoned his "neutral" stand and began sending massive amounts of aid directly to the French forces in Vietnam.

When Dwight Eisenhower became president in 1953, he increased the U.S. support. Altogether, the United States provided more than $2 billion in financial aid and military supplies. But it was not enough. In March 1954 a large force of Communist guerrillas surrounded French troops at Dien Bien Phu (dyen-byen-FOO), a valley in northwestern Vietnam. A fifty-six-day siege followed. On May 7 the French surrendered. The shock of that defeat led France to accept a negotiated end to the war.

The Geneva Accords of 1954 granted Vietnam its independence and divided the country into a Communist North and non-Communist South. Vietnam would be reunited after national elections, scheduled for 1956. But the agreement brought only a temporary truce. By leaving the most important issue unsettled—who would govern all of Vietnam—it had simply planted the seeds for further conflict. Within five years North and South Vietnam would be locked in bitter combat. This time the commitment to halt the spread of Communism would plunge the United States into the longest, most controversial war in its history.

One

America Makes a Commitment

You have a row of dominoes set up, you knock over the first one, and what will happen to the last one is the certainty that it will go over very quickly.

—PRESIDENT DWIGHT EISENHOWER, APRIL 7, 1954

Building a Nation

The "domino theory" spelled out by President Eisenhower just before the French defeat at Dien Bien Phu would shape U.S. policy in Vietnam for the next twenty years. Eisenhower and the three presidents who followed him were determined not to let the nations of Southeast Asia fall to Communism. They would use "all available means" to build up South Vietnam as a barrier to Communist expansion and a proving ground for democracy.

South Vietnam's leader was Ngo Dinh Diem (no-din-zee-EM). A fiercely anti-Communist nationalist, Diem was elected president in 1955 with a suspiciously

Good Guys and Bad Guys

After France's disastrous defeat in Vietnam, how could the United States believe it would fare better? One answer may be found in the conviction—especially widespread after U.S. victories in World War II—that Americans had the spirit, know-how, and resources to accomplish *anything*. U.S. leaders also seemed to believe they would succeed because, unlike the French, who had fought to maintain a colony, they had noble, unselfish goals. The United States did not intend to occupy Vietnam, only to liberate it from Communism.

Ogden Williams served as an adviser to South Vietnam's President Diem in the late 1950s. Years later, he reflected on the sense of mission that inspired Americans in Vietnam during the Cold War years.

> *Our idea in Vietnam was: This is a new nation being born. It has to be something. And naturally, we Americans were convinced that the "something" should be our system of representative government, the best in the world. . . . In those days, when you had U.S. military advisers and that's all, no combat troops, these guys would fall in love not only with the country but also with their Vietnamese unit and their job. . . . They were helping to build a little professional army which had a mission against a ruthless, cruel, determined, well-organized enemy. It was quite clear that there were good guys and bad guys. And the good guys needed help.*

large 98 percent of the vote. In Saigon, South Vietnam's capital, 405,000 registered voters somehow managed to cast more than 605,000 ballots. U.S. leaders might question Diem's methods, but they admired his drive, his patriotism, and especially his stand against Communism. In 1956, when he refused to allow the nationwide elections called for by the Geneva Accords, the United States backed his decision. It was obvious that the popular Communist leader Ho Chi Minh would win any real election—and just as clear that neither side would allow a free vote.

Between 1955 and 1961 the United States poured more than $2 billion into Diem's government. Some of the money went into strengthening the country's economy. Most was spent organizing, equipping, and training a South Vietnamese army. To U.S. observers, the results looked encouraging. The streets of Saigon filled with new cars, new businesses, and prosperous-looking shoppers. More than 200,000 well-armed Vietnamese troops stood ready to defend the peace. Some Americans called Diem a "miracle man" who had saved his country from Communism, and *Newsweek* magazine praised him as "one of the ablest free Asian

A U.S. military adviser trains a South Vietnamese soldier in rifle handling and the use of camouflage.

leaders." But in reality, South Vietnam's government was unstable, unpopular, and far from free.

"Although he professes to believe in representative government and democracy," observed a U.S. intelligence report, "Diem is convinced that the Vietnamese are not ready for such a political system and that he must rule with a firm hand." While South Vietnam's government had the outward appearance of a democracy, Diem alone made all the decisions. He appointed family members to all of the important government posts. He sent tens of thousands of people who criticized his policies to forced-labor camps. Diem also was indifferent to the needs of South Vietnam's peasants, who made up 90 percent of the country's population. His government's "reforms" included abolishing traditional village councils and taking away much of the peasants' land. Corrupt, inefficient local officials often stole what little the people had left.

In North Vietnam Ho Chi Minh's government was even harsher. After the country's division, Ho had established a Communist dictatorship, seizing all private property, establishing control of education and the press, and ruthlessly wiping out all opposition. In his brutal land reform program, thousands of "rich peasants" were executed for the "crime" of owning as little as one acre of land. Despite these excesses, Ho continued to enjoy widespread support, especially among his former guerrilla fighters. Unlike Diem, the Communist leader knew how to use persuasion, propaganda, and promises of a better future to inspire loyalty and obedience.

Thousands of Ho's guerrillas had settled in South Vietnam after the war with France. As discontent with Diem grew, they took up arms again, waging a campaign of kidnappings and violence against government officials. In 1959 the North Vietnamese Communists began to support the resistance movement with soldiers and supplies smuggled down a rough jungle path called the Ho Chi Minh Trail. A year later, the Southern rebels formed the National Liberation Front (NLF), a resistance organization directed from North Vietnam's capital, Hanoi. President Diem dismissed the NLF's members as "Vietnamese Commies," or Vietcong. In fact, the group included not only Ho's Communist supporters but also thousands of non-Communist peasants and other South Vietnamese committed to ending Diem's repressive rule.

The violence quickly escalated. By the end of 1960, the Saigon government was in such "serious danger," reported U.S. ambassador Elbridge Durbrow, that only "prompt and even drastic action" could save it.

Opposing the Foe

In 1961 President John F. Kennedy took office, pledging to "pay any price, bear any burden, . . . support any friend, oppose any foe to assure the survival and the success of liberty." Kennedy believed that the United States was entering the most perilous period in its history. The "red tide of Communism" was on the rise. America's very survival depended on its ability to defend freedom "in its hour of maximum danger."

In Vietnam President Diem's pro-Western government was clearly a "friend" and the Hanoi dictatorship a "foe." Kennedy increased the U.S. commitment, sending more money and weapons to South Vietnam. The number of American military advisers climbed from 900 to 16,000. Some of the president's aides recommended sending in combat troops, too, but Kennedy rejected that idea. "The troops will march in," he predicted, "the bands will play, the crowds will cheer, and in four days everyone will have forgotten. Then we will be told we have to send in more troops."

THE AMERICANS WHO WERE SENT TO HELP THE SOUTH VIETNAMESE ARMY DURING THE KENNEDY ADMINISTRATION WERE NOT SUPPOSED TO ENGAGE IN COMBAT. HOWEVER, THEY OFTEN FACED DANGER AS THEY TRAINED AND LED VIETNAMESE TROOPS AND RECOVERED THE WOUNDED AND DEAD AFTER BATTLES. AMONG THOSE KILLED IN 1963 WAS U.S. ARMY HEL-ICOPTER CREWMAN JAMES MCANDREW. AFTER MCANDREW'S SISTER, BOBBIE LOU PENDERGRASS, WROTE TO THE PRESIDENT FOR HELP IN UNDERSTANDING HER BROTHER'S SACRIFICE, KENNEDY SENT THIS COMPASSIONATE REPLY, EXPLAINING THE REASONS BEHIND AMERICAN INVOLVEMENT IN VIETNAM.*

March 6, 1963

Dear Mrs. Pendergrass:
I would like to express to you my deep and sincere sympathy in the loss of your brother. . . .

The questions which you posed in your letter can, I believe, best be answered by real-izing why your brother—and other American men—went to Viet Nam in the first place.
. . .

*You can read Bobbie Lou Pendergrass's letter to President Kennedy in this book's companion volume, *Letters from the Homefront: The Vietnam War.*

Americans are in Viet Nam because we have determined that this country must not fall under Communist domination. Ever since Viet Nam was divided, the Viet Namese have fought valiantly to maintain their independence in the face of the continuing threat from the North. Shortly after the division eight years ago it became apparent that they could not be successful in their defense without extensive assistance from other nations of the Free World community.

In the late summer of 1955, with the approval of President Eisenhower, an Advisory Group was established in Viet Nam to provide them with adequate weapons and equipment and training in basic military skills which are essential to survival in the battlefield. Even with this help, the situation grew steadily worse under the pressure of the Viet Cong. By 1961 it became apparent that . . . the Communist attempt to take over Viet Nam, is only part of a larger plan for bringing the entire area of Southeast Asia under their domination. Though it is only a small part of the area geographically, Viet Nam is now the most crucial.

If Viet Nam should fall, it will indicate to the people of Southeast Asia that complete Communist domination of their part of the world is almost inevitable. Your brother was in Viet Nam because the threat to the Viet Namese people is, in the long run, a threat to the Free World community, and ultimately a threat to us also. For when freedom is destroyed in one country, it is threatened throughout the world. . . .

I believe if you can see this as he must have seen it, you will believe as he must have believed, that he did not die in vain. Forty-five American soldiers, including your brother, have given their lives in Viet Nam. In their sacrifice, they have earned the eternal gratitude of this Nation and other free men throughout the world. . . .

Sincerely,
John F. Kennedy

Despite U.S. support, the situation in South Vietnam continued to deteriorate. Antigovernment violence increased, and the Diem administration became even more isolated, ineffective, and brutal. In the spring of 1963, the worst turmoil yet erupted over the repression of Buddhism, Vietnam's dominant religion, by Diem, who was a Catholic. Buddhists staged massive demonstrations. Several monks drew worldwide attention to the crisis by setting fire to themselves on the streets of Saigon. After months of chaos a group of South Vietnamese army generals began

Buddhist monk Quang Duc burns himself to death in Saigon in June 1963. This was the first of several suicide protests against the South Vietnamese government's harsh treatment of Buddhists.

plotting a military takeover. Convinced that the war would never be won while Diem was in power, the Kennedy administration quietly signaled its approval.

On November 1, 1963, South Vietnamese troops surrounded the presidential palace in Saigon. The next day Diem was captured and shot to death by the opposition forces. Three weeks later, Kennedy himself was assassinated in Dallas, Texas. Vice President Lyndon B. Johnson assumed the presidency, inheriting a nation in shock and mourning, along with what he called "that bitch of a war" in Vietnam.

Toward a Wider War

President Johnson devoted his first months in office to building confidence in his leadership and shaping his "Great Society," a sweeping program designed to fight poverty and ensure civil rights for all Americans. But even as he concentrated on homefront affairs, the nagging problem of Vietnam kept intruding. Following Diem's overthrow, one military government after another seized power in South Vietnam. Meanwhile, the Vietcong attacks grew even bolder. The North Vietnamese poured men and materials down the Ho Chi Minh Trail, which they had built up into a major supply network. By fueling the rise in terrorism, the Communists hoped to force South Vietnam's collapse and America's withdrawal.

Determined not to let that happen, President Johnson stepped up the military and economic aid. Increasingly, his advisers urged "bolder actions" that would strike directly at the Communist North. The president agreed, but he knew that the American people would never accept a widening of the war without a clear cause. Then, in the summer of 1964, an incident in the waters off North Vietnam gave him the excuse he needed.

On August 4 the U.S. destroyer *Maddox,* on patrol in the Tonkin Gulf, radioed that it was under attack by enemy gunboats. The initial reports turned out to be unreliable and most likely wrong. Nevertheless, Johnson seized the opportunity to ask Congress for a resolution supporting any actions he might consider necessary to defend U.S. interests in Vietnam. The Tonkin Gulf Resolution gave the president authority "to take all necessary measures to repel any armed attack against the forces of the United States and to prevent further aggression."

Johnson used the broad powers granted by the resolution to order Operation Rolling Thunder. On March 2, 1965, U.S. warplanes began striking at military and industrial targets throughout North Vietnam. A few days later, the president sent the first American combat troops to South Vietnam. The mission of these 3,500 marines was to protect the U.S. air base at Da Nang. Maxwell Taylor, the new American ambassador to South Vietnam, warned that the troops were just "the nose of the camel"—once the nose got into the tent, it would be impossible to keep the whole camel out. Events soon proved him right.

In April 1965 President Johnson authorized 40,000 more troops and approved a "change of mission" for the men, from defense alone to "their more active use" in

Marines of the Ninth Expeditionary Brigade—the first U.S. combat troops in Vietnam—race ashore at Da Nang in March 1965.

offensive operations. By July, more than 100,000 U.S. troops were in Vietnam; by the year's end, nearly 185,000. The war had been "Americanized." From this point on, it was no longer a strictly Vietnamese conflict but an American war, directed by U.S. military leaders and fought largely by U.S. troops.

WHILE MOST OF PRESIDENT LYNDON JOHNSON'S ADVISERS RECOMMENDED THE USE OF AIR STRIKES AND GROUND FORCES IN VIETNAM, UNDERSECRETARY OF STATE GEORGE BALL CHALLENGED THOSE POLICIES. BALL HAD STUDIED THE AIR CAMPAIGNS DIRECTED AGAINST GERMANY DURING WORLD WAR II AND HAD FOUND THAT THE BOMBINGS HAD LITTLE EFFECT ON THAT COUNTRY'S WAR INDUSTRIES. HE ALSO TALKED EXTENSIVELY WITH FRENCH PRESIDENT CHARLES DE GAULLE, WHO WARNED THAT THE UNITED STATES WAS ON THE VERGE OF REPEATING THE MISTAKES FRANCE HAD MADE IN VIETNAM. SOON AFTER THE INTRODUCTION OF U.S. COMBAT TROOPS, BALL WROTE THIS MEMO URGING JOHNSON TO SEEK A PEACE SETTLEMENT WHILE COMPROMISE WAS STILL POSSIBLE. HIS WARNINGS OF THE "TERRIBLE COSTS" AHEAD WERE IGNORED, AND HE RESIGNED THE FOLLOWING YEAR.

1 July 1965 Memorandum for the President from George Ball

The South Vietnamese are losing the war to the Viet Cong. No one can assure you that we can beat the Viet Cong or even force them to the conference table on our terms, no matter how many hundred thousand . . . troops we deploy.

No one has demonstrated that a [U.S.] ground force of whatever size can win a guerrilla war—which is at the same time a civil war between Asians—in jungle terrain in the midst of a population that refuses cooperation to the [U.S.] forces (and the South Vietnamese) and thus provides a great intelligence advantage to the other side. . . .

The decision you face now, therefore, is crucial. Once large numbers of U.S. troops are committed to direct combat, they will begin to take heavy casualties in a war they are ill-equipped to fight in a non-cooperative if not downright hostile countryside.

Once we suffer large casualties, we will have started a well-nigh [nearly] irreversible process. Our involvement will be so great that we cannot—without national humiliation—stop short of achieving our complete objectives. Of the two possibilities I think humiliation would be more likely than the achievement of our objectives—even after we have paid terrible costs. . . .

In my judgment, if we act before we commit substantial U.S. troops to combat in South Vietnam we can, by accepting some short-term costs, avoid what may well be a long-term catastrophe.

Two

Into the Tunnel

It's not like the San Francisco Forty-niners on one side of the field and the Cincinnati Bengals on the other. It's just not like that. The enemy is all around you. . . . You never knew who was the enemy and who was the friend.

—MARINE VETERAN EDWARD BANKS

Mission: Search and Destroy

The first wave of American combat troops went to Vietnam eager—or at least willing—to serve their country in a worthwhile cause. Army rifleman Frank McCarthy was a "gung ho" patriot who saw U.S. armed forces as "the defenders of freedom and liberty throughout the world." Infantryman Marc Leepson "didn't know much about what was happening in Vietnam . . . but I figured that if my country was involved, the cause must be just." All the men looked forward to an early victory. After all, how could a small, "backward" nation of peasant farmers stand up to America's vast military might?

American combat soldiers in camouflage patrol the jungles of South Vietnam.

The realities of combat were different from anything they expected. For a generation raised on World War II movies with dashing heroes who charged into battle and wiped out the enemy almost single-handedly, Vietnam was bewildering. This was a guerrilla war, with no clear battlefront. Large-scale engagements pitting one army against another for control of territory were rare. Instead, Americans waged a daily struggle against a faceless enemy that could strike anytime, anywhere.

FRANK MCCARTHY OF PHILADELPHIA WENT TO VIETNAM WITH THE ARMY INFANTRY IN OCTOBER 1965, PROUD TO JOIN THE FIGHT AGAINST THE FORCES OF COMMUNISM. LIKE MANY YOUNG SOLDIERS, HOWEVER, MCCARTHY SOON FOUND THAT HE WAS UNPREPARED FOR THE BRUTAL REALITIES OF COMBAT. BY THE TIME HE RETURNED HOME IN MARCH 1967, MCCARTHY HAD BEEN WOUNDED FOUR TIMES AND ALL BUT SIX MEN OUT OF HIS ORIGINAL THIRTY-TWO-MAN PLATOON HAD BEEN KILLED OR SERIOUSLY INJURED. YEARS LATER, HE REFLECTED ON HIS INTRODUCTION TO GUERRILLA WARFARE IN VIETNAM.

We were trained to do a mop-up operation in a country the size of Washington State in about a year, then come home. This was another confrontation with the Communists around the world. . . . We truly believed that we could do the job. . . .

The first time I ever saw any of our own guys get it was on our third patrol. I was walking point [lead man] and Lenny and Steve were behind me. A mine went off and wiped out the eleven guys behind them.

The guys in my unit were absolutely enraged because for the previous year we had all been very close. Every weekend our families would visit. We knew guys' wives, mothers, and fathers, their kids. And when they died it enraged us. We wanted to find the VC [Vietcong] and kill them. But at that point it was very difficult to find them. They were ghosts. They would hit us with a mortar, plant a booby trap or mine. But you'd never see anybody.

The first time we saw them was a battle going on at a South Vietnamese . . . camp. We went out in the morning. I was walking point for the battalion and was the first person into the area. The VC regiment had run over the camp and killed three hundred South Vietnamese. And there were about four hundred Viet Cong dead. So seven hundred to a thousand bodies were spewed all over the ground. I was pretty numbed by it all.

I had seen every World War II movie as a kid and loved them all. But walking amongst the bodies that were intertwined the way they died in hand-to-hand fighting . . . a Viet Cong with a bayonet in his chest clutching a South Vietnamese with bullets in his back . . . that was my first real shocker.

"The way we move without contact," wrote Lieutenant Don Jacques of the U.S. Marines, "you begin to wonder if the VC are even out there. And all the time you know they are. The great frustration is that they don't come out and fight." Jacques was describing a "search-and-destroy" mission. American combat troops devoted most of their time to this type of operation. Helicoptered deep into the countryside, the men plodded through the steamy jungles and flooded rice paddies for days or weeks, searching for enemy bases and supply areas. Each infantryman, or "grunt," was weighed down by fifty to seventy pounds of equipment. Stifling heat, rain, snakes, leeches, and biting insects compounded the misery. "We live in mud and rain," platoon leader Frederick Downs wrote to his wife.

> I'm so sick of rain that it is sometimes unbearable. At night the mosquitoes plague me while I'm lying on the ground with my poncho wrapped around me. The rain drips on me until I go to sleep from exhaustion. This continues day after day until one wonders how much the human body can stand.

An exhausted GI tries to grab a nap. On search-and-destroy missions soldiers averaged fewer than four hours of sleep a night.

The Vietcong laced the fields and trails with lethal mines and booby traps. One wrong step could mean crippling injury or death. There was also the constant danger of sniper fire or ambush. In the tangled jungle growth, it was impossible to see more than a few feet. At any moment the silence might be broken by a sudden burst of fire. For infantryman Mark Smith combat was almost a relief.

> It was better to get into a fight than just walk around sweating. . . . When you made contact with the enemy, you went from the most horrible boredom to the most intense excitement. . . . Someone was trying to kill you and you were trying to kill someone, and it was like every thrill hitting you all at once.

Most firefights were brief—a few minutes of blinding, deafening chaos before the Vietcong faded back under cover. A patrol that came under heavy fire radioed for artillery and helicopter gunships to blast the enemy. Medevac (medical evacuation) helicopters picked up the wounded and dead. Transport helicopters returned patrols to their base camp for a few days' rest. Then it was back into the field for another miserable, frustrating, deadly search-and-destroy mission.

MEDICS—SOLDIERS WITH SPECIAL TRAINING IN FIRST AID—ACCOMPANIED INFANTRY UNITS ON PATROL. ROBERT TILLQUIST OF CONNECTICUT WENT TO VIETNAM AS AN ARMY MEDIC IN AUGUST 1965. HE WAS KILLED THREE MONTHS LATER WHILE TREATING A WOUNDED SOLDIER DURING A SEARCH-AND-DESTROY MISSION. TWO DAYS EARLIER, TILLQUIST HAD SENT THIS LETTER TO HIS FORMER HIGH SCHOOL TEACHER, EXPLAINING WHY HE BELIEVED AMERICANS HAD A DUTY TO HELP THE SOUTH VIETNAMESE FIGHT COMMUNISM.

2 Nov. 65

Hello:

Remember me? . . . Your favorite (huh?) student (past tense) is now in Vietnam. . . .

Just as other young men are afraid of dying, so am I. This to me was sufficient reason for my concern for my personal welfare when I was ordered over here with the Airmobile Division by President Johnson. A fear of dying is a great burden to a young man who has not fully tasted all that life has to offer.

So I came over here with many misgivings. I didn't want to come over here, I didn't want to leave the security of my nice comfortable home, or of America. Why should I give up the luxurious life I knew in the States, to come over here and fight, fight for something I didn't really care about?

After only a few weeks here, these and many other questions were answered. Just being here and having contact with these people can tell you many things.

When you see children 6 or 7 years old, with one or more of their limbs brutally amputated. Or orphanages overcrowded with young boys and girls who were forced to watch the massacre of their parents. Or fertile fields that would grow almost any crop, ravaged and destroyed (with the harvest that would have fed the people of the village, laying in the ruins), just to deprive the people of subsistence. When you see this and much more (things to make even the strongest of men cry out in anger, at the outrage of it all) then you understand the reason for your being here.

I came here afraid for my life. Now I would gladly lay down my life for these little (but only in stature) people. They have brave hearts and fight on against a terrible foe. A man who is not proud and willing to help these people, after seeing what they have to fight against, is not much of a man, not much of an American. . . .

Robert A. Tillquist

The Elusive Enemy

One of the greatest frustrations for American soldiers in Vietnam was simply trying to identify the enemy. A rice farmer in his field, a young woman carrying her baby, a boy on his bicycle—all these might be Vietcong sympathizers or even VC themselves. "They all looked alike. They all dressed alike," recalled Captain Edward Banks.

> Here's a woman of twenty-two or twenty-three. She is pregnant, and she tells an interrogator that her husband works in Da Nang and isn't a Vietcong. But she watches your men walk down a trail and get killed or wounded by a booby trap. She knows the booby trap is there, but she doesn't warn them. Maybe she planted it herself.

A GI questions a South Vietnamese woman whose husband is a suspected Vietcong.

Some GIs concluded that all Vietnamese were the enemy—including the people they were supposed to be fighting to defend. Distrust, anger, and fear sometimes led to atrocities. The most notorious of these was the My Lai Massacre of March 1968. In that shocking incident American troops on a search-and-destroy mission in the South Vietnamese village of My Lai murdered some five hundred unarmed civilians, including old men, women, and children.

Most soldiers never committed acts of violence against civilians. In fact, through a program aimed at "winning the hearts and minds" of the Vietnamese people, hundreds of GIs distributed supplies to schools and orphanages, built roads and bridges, and provided agricultural assistance and medical care. Vietnam veteran George Firehammer remembered one medic who cared for "a Vietnamese woman in her seventies who was suffering with a high temperature. We were in an ambush site near a village, and he ministered to this woman all night until her fever broke." Nevertheless, day-to-day military actions far outweighed all the good individual soldiers did.

Marine veteran William Ehrhart recalled a typical mission in the spring of 1965, when his company was ordered to search a group of villages. The peasants were "herded like cattle into a barbed-wire compound" so that interrogators could question them about guerrilla activities. Meanwhile, the marines wrecked their homes, took their rice, and killed their livestock to keep food out of enemy hands. "If they weren't pro-Vietcong before we got there," observed Ehrhart, "they sure as hell were by the time we left."

WILLIAM EHRHART SERVED WITH THE U.S. MARINES IN VIETNAM FROM 1967 TO 1968. TODAY HE IS ONE OF THE MOST WIDELY KNOWN VETERAN WRITERS AND POETS. EHRHART'S POEM "GUERRILLA WAR" EXPRESSED THE GI'S FRUSTRATION IN A WORLD WHERE INNOCENCE AND GUILT WERE HOPELESSLY MUDDLED AND THE ENEMY SEEMED TO BE EVERYWHERE.

It's practically impossible
to tell civilians
from the Vietcong.

Nobody wears uniforms.
They all talk
the same language
(and you couldn't understand them
even if they didn't).

They tape grenades
inside their clothes,
and carry satchel charges
in their market baskets.

Even their women fight;
and young boys,
and girls.

It's practically impossible
to tell civilians from the Vietcong;

after awhile,
you quit trying.

Stalemate and Frustration

The strategy behind the search-and-destroy operations was called attrition. In a war of attrition, an army tries to wear down its opponent through constant attacks and harassment. Eventually, the enemy becomes so weak and weary that it decides to give up the fight.

While most search-and-destroy missions involved small combat units, U.S. military leaders also hoped to weaken the Communists' fighting spirit by demonstrating America's superiority in a full-scale engagement. They got their first chance in late 1965. On October 19 three North Vietnamese regiments attacked a U.S. Army camp in the Ia Drang (yah-DRAHN) Valley of Vietnam's Central Highlands region. The Americans struck back, forcing the attackers to retreat and then pursuing them deep into the surrounding jungles. Over the next five weeks, a series of fierce battles killed 305 Americans and some 3,500 North Vietnamese.

After Ia Drang the Communists avoided major battles. By 1967 the war seemed to be a stalemate. The guerrilla attacks and the search-and-destroy operations continued, while the death toll on both sides mounted. Still, the Communists could not defeat South Vietnam and its U.S. allies, and the Americans and South Vietnamese could not force North Vietnam and the Vietcong to give up.

An exhausted GI rests beside the trenches after combat with North Vietnamese forces. Following the fierce Battle of Ia Drang in October 1965, major engagements between the Americans and North Vietnamese were rare.

"We'd take [a] territory, then we'd pick up and go home," recalled marine veteran John Catterson. "Two weeks later we could be fighting the same group on the same hill." U.S. forces were stretched too thin to defend every area cleared of the enemy. Often the Vietcong simply slipped back in after the Americans left. What was the point, discouraged GIs asked, of risking their lives taking and retaking the same scrap of land?

Adding to the soldiers' frustration were the limitations placed on them by the Rules of Engagement. These were directives handed down by top military authorities, intended to limit injuries and property losses to civilians. The Rules said that U.S. ground troops could not follow the enemy into neighboring countries. "Chasing a VC regiment right up to the Cambodian border and having to stop was insanity," argued infantryman Frank McCarthy. Allowing the Communists a safe haven to rest up and resupply "gave the enemy the advantage of striking us anytime they wanted to."

Also discouraging was the poor performance of the South Vietnamese army. Some of the best units fought bravely and well. In general, though, the South's soldiers were poorly paid and poorly led. GIs complained that their Vietnamese allies went out of their way to avoid a fight. During combat, they might run or fire blind-

Troops at the Rear

For every American "in the field" in Vietnam, there were five or six "in the rear"—military personnel stationed outside combat areas to support the fighting troops. Support personnel performed hundreds of different jobs: driving trucks, fixing engines, building barracks, cooking meals, sorting mail, ordering supplies. They faced far fewer dangers than the combat soldiers. In a war without clear front lines, however, even a typist is never completely safe. Regardless of their assignment, three-quarters of all U.S. troops in Vietnam came under enemy fire at some time, and more than half saw a fellow soldier wounded or killed.

ly. Sometimes they abused or stole from the villagers, angering civilians who were already alienated from their government and its U.S. allies.

That anger could be one of the most frustrating parts of the Americans' whole confusing, contradictory mission. Young men who had come to Vietnam as saviors found themselves cast as villains. To "save" a village from the Vietcong, they might be ordered to destroy it completely, burning homes and property and driving the people off their land. Forced into overcrowded cities or filthy refugee camps, the embittered civilians made ready converts to the Communist cause. "It began to seem crazy," said William Ehrhart. "Maybe we Americans weren't the guys in white hats, riding white horses. Maybe we shouldn't be in Vietnam."

The War in the Air

Combat pilots in Vietnam shared many of the frustrations of the fighting troops on the ground. "Under the Rules of Engagement," complained air force pilot Mark Berent, "we were forced to fight the war with a hand tied behind our back, one eye blinded, and only half a pocket full of ammunition."

The Rules for air combat limited the targets aircraft could hit. To pilots, these limits often seemed not only senseless but dangerous. For example, bombers might be forbidden to hit a missile-launching site or a convoy of trucks carrying war supplies because the targets were near the Chinese border. Later, said Berent, the pilots could be shot down from "sites that they had watched being built," while the supplies that had been left untouched "contributed to American deaths on the battlefield."

When pilots did hit a target, the North Vietnamese and Vietcong quickly rebuilt. Pilots risked their lives again and again taking out the same road, factory, or bridge. Dick Rutan, who flew 325 missions in Vietnam, recalled that he

> never one time saw a road closed or cut. . . . I'd go up there and I'd see a major strike going in. Pulverize the road. Wouldn't even be a road left. I'd come back later and all of a sudden, out would come a little bulldozer going right over the bomb craters. Didn't hardly slow it down.

By late 1967, the United States had dropped nearly two million tons of bombs on Vietnam, causing hundreds of millions of dollars in damage. The massive air strikes never achieved their main objective, however: stopping the flow of men and arms to South Vietnam and breaking the spirit of the North Vietnamese people.

ROBERT KIRK WAS A U.S. AIR FORCE PILOT WHO FLEW 197 COMBAT MISSIONS IN THE F-4 PHANTOM FIGHTER-BOMBER. LATER HE REFLECTED ON BOTH THE POSITIVE AND NEGATIVE SIDES OF HIS SERVICE, INCLUDING THE SATISFACTION OF HELPING THE TROOPS ON THE GROUND AND THE DANGERS, CONTRADICTIONS, AND TERRIBLE INHUMANITY OF WAR.

Some missions just weren't worth flying. . . . For me they more or less fit into two categories: the worthless jobs, the bombing runs on trails, . . . and the important jobs, helping friendly ground troops. We would scramble, work out of the alert shack in twelve-hour shifts, fly in support of ground troops in contact. These were important missions! That's the way I felt. When we knew there were troops in trouble, there was absolutely no question about us coming to help. . . .

Choices. It came down to making choices. The whole war experience was very personal. I was a patriot, I loved my country, I would fight. I was a Christian, I believed the Bible, I believed it was wrong to kill, how could I kill? . . .

The absurdity of it all hit me hardest one in-country mission. . . . We were hitting a suspected troop concentration in a bunker complex. We had made several runs when the FAC [forward air controller] told us an old man had walked out of one of the bunkers and was sitting on a log. He had staggered out of a bunker into full view, just sitting there (my guess dying), with all this destruction around him. I don't know what was going through his mind, but I felt sorrow for him.

The FAC came back on the radio and was going crazy. He was shouting, "Kill him, kill him!" Our wingman made a run at the old man with a 20-mm cannon. He opened up and somehow missed him. What must the old man be thinking? He's just trying to die, and here are these crazies risking a two-million-dollar aircraft and two pilots to kill an old man. It was ludicrous. The FAC screamed again, "You missed! Kill him, kill him!" It was madness. I came on the radio and said, "Let's go home."

The Turning Point

By the end of 1967, there were 485,000 American troops in Vietnam. More than 16,000 had been killed in action. Meanwhile, the Vietcong forces were larger and more active than ever. In December President Johnson authorized more troops and widened the list of bombing targets. "We are not going to yield," the president declared. "We are going to wind up with a peace with honor."

Then came a series of events that marked the turning point of the war.

On January 21, 1968, the North Vietnamese assaulted the U.S. Marine base at Khe Sanh (kay-SAHN). For the next seventy-eight days, 6,000 marines battled to hold off a force of more than 20,000 attackers. The besieged troops

A combat medic treats the wounded after a deadly firefight in late 1965. More than 358,000 GIs were wounded or killed during America's involvement in Vietnam.

braved hunger and thirst, constant artillery and sniper fire, and desperate hand-to-hand fighting. More than 200 Americans and thousands of North Vietnamese lost their lives.

With all its costs the Battle of Khe Sanh may have only been a ruse to draw U.S. forces away from South Vietnam's cities, in preparation for a much larger attack. That offensive began on January 31, at the start of Tet, the Vietnamese lunar New Year. In the early morning hours, some 70,000 North Vietnamese and Vietcong troops launched coordinated assaults on more than 150 major cities, towns, and military bases throughout South Vietnam. In Saigon Communist commandos held the U.S. Embassy grounds for six hours before they were all killed or captured.

Elsewhere in Vietnam American and South Vietnamese troops subdued the Communists in battles lasting a few hours or a few days. The longest and bloodiest face-off took place in the ancient imperial capital of Hue (hway). There fierce house-to-house fighting continued for twenty-five days. As marine commander Myron Harrington reported, the Americans engaged the enemy

> in a face-to-face, eyeball-to-eyeball confrontation. Sometimes they were only twenty or thirty yards from us, and once we killed a sniper only ten yards away. After a while, survival was the name of the game as you sat there in the semidarkness, with the fighting going on constantly, like at a rifle range.

Six hundred Americans and South Vietnamese lost their lives in the fierce battle to recapture Hue. Adding to the horror was the civilian death toll. Soon after the Communists overran the city, they began rounding up and executing an estimated 5,700 government workers, teachers, doctors, priests, foreign residents, and other "antirevolutionaries." Many people were shot or beaten to death and thrown in mass graves. Some were buried alive.

Overall the Tet Offensive proved to be a devastating defeat for the Communists. They lost most of their attacking army, including so many Vietcong that the guerrilla forces never fully recovered. But in the United States, Tet didn't look like much of a victory. Military leaders had been telling war-weary Americans that "the light at the end of the tunnel" was in sight. Now news reports and TV images of Tet's widespread, savage fighting made those promises look like lies. Stunned and outraged, the American people turned overwhelmingly against the war.

On March 31 President Johnson announced that he was sharply limiting the air strikes on North Vietnam as "the first in what I hope will be a series of steps toward peace." Hounded by critics on all sides, Johnson also declared that he would not seek reelection. A new president would inherit a troubled America, along with a new challenge in Vietnam: not how to win the war but how to withdraw without seeming to lose it.

Three

Minorities and Women in the War

The government was using us blacks. . . . At that particular time, most of the whites depended on the brothers to fight. That's how it got to be. . . . Every brother knew that. . . . [Our] thing was, "Don't let them use you all the way into the grave."

—ARMY VETERAN STANLEY GOFF

"A Black Man's Fight"

"In Vietnam," observed one journalist, "Uncle Sam was an equal opportunity employer." Those who served included both men and women from a range of ethnic groups: white, black, Hispanic, Asian American, Native American.

Black men especially did more than their share of the fighting and dying. Vietnam was the first war in which African Americans served in a fully integrated military—a privilege for which they paid a high price. "A few of us black soldiers," recalled infantry veteran Robert Holcomb,

An infantryman rescues a fellow soldier wounded in heavy enemy shelling. Despite racial con-flicts, GIs worked together as a team during combat operations.

were able to get into positions where we could have some freedom, make our lives a little better. . . . But most blacks couldn't, because they didn't have the skills. So they were put in the jobs that were the most dangerous, the hardest, or just the most undesirable.

In 1965 African Americans made up about 10 percent of all U.S. troops in Vietnam but more than 20 percent of combat deaths. That was because black soldiers were much more likely than whites to be assigned to combat units. Some infantry units were 50 percent black. And more often than not, it was the black grunt who served as "point man" or carried the patrol's machine gun—the two most vital and hazardous jobs. Black soldiers also were punished for misconduct more severely than whites, and they were rarely promoted or recognized for their accomplishments.

Resentment over these inequities led to tension between black and white soldiers, which sometimes exploded in violence. The racial incidents didn't happen on patrol, when grunts depended on one another for survival. But in the rear and at the base camps where troops "stood down" between missions, it almost began to seem as if there were two wars: one between the Americans and the Communists, another between black and white soldiers.

In 1967 military commanders took steps to reduce African-American casualties. Fewer blacks were assigned to combat units, more to support jobs in the rear. For many black servicemen, however, the changes never erased the feeling that Vietnam was "a white man's war, a black man's fight."

RICHARD FORD OF WASHINGTON, D.C., SERVED WITH AN ARMY INFANTRY SPECIAL FORCES UNIT IN VIETNAM FROM 1967 TO 1968. BETWEEN MISSIONS HIS UNIT RESTED UP AT A CAMP AT NHA TRANG. AFTER THE WAR FORD RECALLED THE ANGER HE AND HIS COMRADES FELT TOWARD THE WHITE SOLDIERS WHO WERE "IN THE BACK HAVING A BIG SHOW" WHILE BLACKS WERE GETTING "BLOWN AWAY" IN THE FIELD.

The racial incidents didn't happen in the field. Just when we went to the back. It wasn't so much that they were against us. It was just that we felt that we were being taken advantage of, 'cause it seemed like more blacks in the field than in the rear.

In the rear we saw a bunch of rebel [Civil War Confederate] flags. They didn't mean nothing by the rebel flag. It was just saying we for the South. It didn't mean that they hated blacks. But after you in the field, you took the flags very personally.

One time we saw these flags in Nha Trang on the MP [military police] barracks. They was playing hillbilly music. Had their shoes off dancing. Had nice, pretty bunks. Mosquito nets over top the bunks. And had the nerve to have these camouflaged covers. Air conditioning. . . . We just came out the jungles. We dirty, we smelly, hadn't shaved. We just went off. Said, "Y'all the real enemy. We stayin' here." We turned the bunks over, started tearing up the stereo. They just ran out. Next morning, they shipped us back up.

In the field, we had the utmost respect for each other, because when a fire fight is going on and everybody is facing north, you don't want to see nobody looking around south. If you was a member of the Ku Klux Klan, you didn't tell nobody.

The Black Power Movement

The conflicts among the troops in Vietnam mirrored racial tensions on the American homefront. More than a decade earlier, the civil rights movement had begun to challenge segregation and discrimination. Led by the Reverend Martin Luther King, Jr., civil rights workers used nonviolent protests such as boycotts, sit-ins, and marches to press for equal rights and opportunities. Peaceful protesters often were harassed, jailed, or beaten. Over time many became angry and impatient with the lack of progress. Some began calling for "black power" and a "black revolution." Beginning in the summer of 1965, their frustrations ignited race riots in

Artillerymen raise clenched fists as a sign of "black power" at an American army base near the border with North Vietnam.

dozens of American cities, causing millions of dollars in damage and hundreds of deaths.

By the late 1960s, young black men were bringing their increasingly militant outlook to Vietnam. "A barrier had sprung up," recalled infantry officer Ken Moorefield.

> For example, blacks had their own club in the battalion base camp. Whites were not welcome there. . . . Blacks felt alienated and isolated. They were finding it harder and harder to identify with this war. Back in the United States, before they ever came into the army, the Black Power movement was emphasizing their differences.

Following the assassination of Martin Luther King on April 4, 1968, an outburst of racial violence rocked dozens of U.S. cities and military bases. In Vietnam the incidents ranged from fistfights to full-scale riots.

Air force security guard Don Browne was stationed in Saigon. "When I heard that Martin Luther King was assassinated," he remembered, "my first inclination was to run out and punch the first white guy I saw." A few days later, Browne and two other black GIs overheard a white soldier complaining that he was "sick and tired" of seeing Dr. King's picture on TV and wished "they'd take that nigger's picture off. . . . We commenced to give him a lesson in when to use that word and when you should not use that word. A physical lesson."

Army veteran Woody Wanamaker witnessed a larger confrontation at an infantry camp north of Saigon in the summer of 1968.

> This infantry unit came in on standdown for two or three days, and there was some incident involving a black and a white at one of the EM [enlisted men's] clubs. It spread into their company area—blacks against whites, whites against Puerto Ricans, blacks against Puerto Ricans. I don't think there was any shooting, but they sure was going at it.

Despite the continuing racial turmoil, injustices, and dangers, the great majority of black GIs performed their duties with skill and courage. Altogether, about

Hispanics: The "Ham in the Sandwich"

About 170,000 Hispanic men served in Vietnam. Whether their origins were Mexican, Cuban, or Puerto Rican, most ended up in the infantry. There they often encountered racist treatment by their fellow soldiers, both white and black. Angel Quintana was a young Puerto Rican who was drafted into the army in 1966. His first contact with racism came at a training camp in Georgia.

> It wasn't only the whites who were racist against us—the blacks were, too. We had problems with both. The blacks took out on us what the whites did to them. We got kicked by both sides. We were the ham in the sandwich. . . . When I finally went [to Vietnam], I was already traumatized. I had such an attitude that when they gave me my rifle, the first people I wanted to shoot weren't the Vietnamese but the people who gave it to me.

Quintana served for seven months with an infantry unit operating around the Ho Chi Minh Trail. He saw nearly every one of his friends badly wounded or killed and was himself wounded by an American mine. When he returned home, he began drinking heavily, "looking for a way to forget." After years of drifting, Quintana overcame his problems and became a counselor at a veterans' center in Newark, New Jersey. One of the lessons he shared with other veterans who used alcohol and drugs as "medicine" to ease their pain was this: "It's stupid, because you're never going to forget. The past is a sickness you can't cure."

275,000 African Americans served in Vietnam; more than 5,700 died in action. Twenty received the Congressional Medal of Honor, the highest American military award for bravery. "Never before," noted historian Clark Smith, "had blacks played the paramount role they did in Vietnam. . . . It is fair to say that the black soldier proved himself equal to the task."

Women in the Combat Zones

Thousands of American women served in Vietnam, both in civilian and military roles. Civilian women worked with the American Red Cross and other charitable organizations and at U.S. government offices. Women in the armed forces included photographers, mapmakers, air traffic controllers, intelligence analysts, secretaries, and interrogators. Eight out of ten of the 7,500 military women in Vietnam were nurses.

Some nurses worked on navy hospital ships or air force medical evacuation planes. Most served in the army, working at either field hospitals in combat zones or at the larger, better-equipped hospitals in the rear. Few were prepared for the horrible injuries and suffering they saw. "Not even working with earthquake victims or in the emergency

The sight of American women in combat gear was extremely rare during the Vietnam War. The great majority of military women faced hardship and danger as nurses and in other medical fields.

room of a big hospital could equal what I saw in a single day in Vietnam," recalled Ruth Sidisin, a nurse at an air force base near Saigon.

The weapons used by both sides were designed to inflict massive, multiple injuries. Patients with gaping wounds and one or more limbs missing were common. Speedy helicopter evacuation and sophisticated medical care made survival possible for severely wounded men who would have died in earlier wars. Army nurse Mary Stout remembered one soldier who had been wounded by a mine.

> He lost both legs at the hip, plus a hand and an arm. And he was blind, had a head injury and lots of internal injuries. . . . That guy we did surgery on—even with all those things wrong, he was still alive. It was absolutely amazing.

LYNDA VAN DEVANTER WAS TWENTY-ONE YEARS OLD WHEN SHE JOINED THE U.S. ARMY NURSE CORPS IN 1968, EAGER TO "GIVE PART OF MYSELF TO KEEP AMERICA GREAT." LIKE MOST OF THE AMERICAN NURSES IN VIETNAM, SHE PUT IN LONG DAYS AND NIGHTS WORKING ON SHATTERED BODIES. HER FEELINGS RANGED FROM LONELINESS, FEAR, AND SORROW TO A GROWING SENSE THAT ALL THE "DEATH, DESTRUCTION, AND MISERY" WERE FOR NOTHING. IN THIS TAPE-RECORDED LETTER SENT TO HER PARENTS IN THE SUMMER OF 1969, VAN DEVANTER EXPRESSED BOTH HER FRUSTRATIONS AND THE SATISFACTION THAT CAME FROM DOING A VITAL JOB UNDER EXTREMELY DEMANDING CONDITIONS.

Hi, Mom and Dad.

I'm too tired to write now, so I figured I'd send you a tape instead. The last couple of weeks have been really bad. Some of our guys have been getting hit pretty hard. We've been working up to eighteen, twenty-four and thirty-six hours at a time for weeks. When we get time off, I just sleep. . . .

You know, it's getting kind of hard to explain my feelings about this whole thing. In the past couple of weeks I've seen a few of my friends come in pretty blown up, guys who've been at our parties or who've been in the hospital before. It's harder when you see it happen to somebody you've known. And over here, you get to know people really fast.

We worked on a couple of guys yesterday who were really banged up. We spent twelve to fourteen hours on each one, and they would have died if it wasn't for the doctors. One of the guys had four holes in his heart. Sometimes, these guys will come into the ER [emergency room] bleeding and they'll look up at you and say, "I must have died. I'm dead, aren't I?"

It's depressing and yet it's almost reassuring at the same time. They know that somebody cares enough to be over here when they don't have to be. I think the thing that's most depressing about the whole situation is the fact that nobody's admitting that something is going wrong over here. . . .

But out of it all, I guess there's some satisfaction for me in knowing that I'm doing a job that's needed. . . . Here, you're always doing something that's necessary. For the first time in my life, I feel like I have to keep going or people might not survive. It's time for me to return to the operating room, so I'd better say good-bye.

Military nurses lived with the dangers of enemy attack, of snipers and rocket fire. They learned to deal with their fear, grief, and anger by bottling up their emotions. Leslie McClusky, who worked at an army hospital in Chu Lai, described the experience as "a total emotional numbing. . . . I did my job well and was able to show compassion, but I worked hard at not feeling compassion."

After their tour in Vietnam, nurses often had a hard time dismantling their emotional walls. Like army veteran Lynda Van Devanter, many spent years making peace with their "ghosts . . . the most painful and most important memories of my life." But along with the pain, most felt a lasting pride in their service. Mary Stout came home believing that "the war was wrong" and carrying a heavy load of "guilt and pain . . . about losing patients, about taking care of people and then having to see them die." Still, she has

> never been ashamed of having volunteered. . . . I think we did wonderful, wonderful work. I can't even imagine anything else I could have done where it would have felt more satisfying. In Vietnam I worked harder than I ever have, and I did more good.

Four

Questions and Confrontations

I was in Vietnam when I first heard about the thousands of people protesting the war in the streets of America. I didn't want to believe it at first—people protesting against us when we were putting our lives on the line for our country. The men in my outfit used to talk about it a lot. How could they do this to us?

—MARINE VETERAN RON KOVIC

A Divided Nation

While American men and women worked, fought, and died in Vietnam, the war was generating its own battles at home. At first, the vast majority of Americans had supported the government's war policies. But in early 1965, after President Johnson sent in the first combat troops, many people began to change their minds.

The earliest antiwar activists, or "doves," included college students and long-time pacifists (people opposed to all wars). They staged peaceful protests borrowed from the civil rights movement—rallies, marches, picket lines, sit-ins. By 1967, the

An antiwar demonstrator pokes fun at Vice President Spiro Agnew, a passionate (and wordy) "hawk" who called the administration's war critics "an effete corps of impudent snobs who characterize themselves as intellectuals."

antiwar movement had widened. Huge rallies in New York, San Francisco, Washington, and other cities were drawing hundreds of thousands of protesters representing all ages, races, and walks of life. After the Tet Offensive in 1968, support for the government's policies dropped even further. Public opinion polls showed that more than half of all Americans believed the long, frustrating war was at a standstill. They had lost confidence in their leaders, and they would not tolerate further losses without some believable promise of success.

Not all Americans joined the antiwar movement. Many believed it was their patriotic duty to stand solidly behind their country, right or wrong. These "hawks" sometimes staged their own rallies to counter the antiwar demonstrations. In May 1967 70,000 hawks marched in New York City, carrying signs reading *Support Our Boys, God Bless Us Patriots,* and *Down with the Reds.*

Opposing the Draft

One of the main targets of antiwar protest was the draft. Nearly two million young men were drafted during the Vietnam years. The system that selected them has been called "a national disgrace."

Every male citizen from the ages of nineteen to twenty-six was eligible for the draft. However, there were plenty of loopholes for well-educated whites from well-to-do families. Many of these young men were granted exemptions or deferments (postponements) by local draft boards, which were nearly always made up of middle-class white men. Others were assigned to stateside service. Also, until December 1971, the law automatically deferred service for college students.

Antiwar activists protested these unfair practices and challenged the government's right to make them serve in a war they opposed. Many picketed and staged sit-ins at local draft boards. Some publicly burned their draft cards. About 150,000 young men fled the country rather than answer the draft call.

Even war supporters became increasingly critical of the inequities in the draft system. In 1969 the government responded to the criticism by instituting a national draft lottery. The lottery used dates plucked from a glass bowl to determine the order of draft selection. A man whose birthday was pulled first became part of the group that would be drafted first. Last, and he was home free—the draft board would almost certainly meet its quota long before he was called.

Although the lottery system was supposed to even the field, many well-off, well-connected young men still found ways to avoid the draft call. According to one study, a high-school dropout from a low-income family was nearly twice as likely as a college graduate to serve in Vietnam. Once there, draftees were far more likely than men who voluntarily enlisted to be assigned to combat units and to be killed in action.

Often hawks objected not only to the antiwar demonstrations but to the demonstrators themselves. Every peace rally included crowds of high school and college students with long, shaggy hair, wearing torn blue jeans, sandals, and "love beads." Young people were in the midst of a "counterculture revolution," questioning the older generation's lifestyle and values. They played loud rock-and-roll music, and they experimented with freer sexual behavior and mind-altering drugs. Young women were also challenging their traditional role as the "weaker sex" and demanding greater opportunities in work and education. To many older Americans, all these forces of change were confusing and threatening. Even those who had begun to question the war found it "very difficult," explained one poll taker, to side with "the Black Panthers, women's liberation, widespread use of drugs, free love, campus radicals . . . [and] long hair."

There were no peace rallies in Vietnam, no rock concerts on shady college campuses. Nevertheless, the antiwar movement and the counterculture had a major impact on young Americans serving far from home, in the war dividing their homeland.

Long hair, tie-dyed T-shirts, ragged blue jeans, and peace symbols were some of the signs of the youthful counterculture during the Vietnam War years.

"We Gotta Get Out of This Place"

Many GIs were outraged by news of the antiwar protests. To Private Richard Marks of the U.S. Marine Corps, the "people opposing the American action in V.N." were "fools. . . . It horrifies and disgusts me to think that the same students that oppose Johnson today will rule the nation tomorrow." Ron Kovic, who enlisted in the marines at age eighteen, recalled that the men in his company swore vengeance against "the hippies and draftcard burners. . . . They would pay if we ever ran into them."

EIGHTEEN-YEAR-OLD RICHARD E. MARKS, WHO JOINED THE MARINE CORPS IN 1964, WAS PROUD OF HIS ROLE IN THE WAR AGAINST COMMUNISM. IN THIS LETTER TO THE EDITOR OF HIS HIGH SCHOOL'S ALUMNI NEWSLETTER, HE EXPRESSED THE BEWILDERMENT MANY SOLDIERS FELT ABOUT THE ANTIWAR MOVEMENT. MARKS WAS KILLED IN COMBAT IN FEBRUARY 1966.

July 7, 1965

Dear Mr. Whiting—

My mother has written and told me that excerps of my letter to you will be printed in the Hackley Journal—it is hard to find words to tell you how wonderful that makes me feel. While at Hackley I often tried to get work put in the Hackley, . . . but none of my work was ever accepted, and now, out of a rainy Vietnamese sky, I'm in print. All I can say is thank you for the honor and priviledge.

I have a question to pose, and it is what is happening to the system of education in the United States? We are reading about people who are opposing the war in Viet Nam, and suggesting we pull American troops out. How can these people (College and University demonstrators) be serious. Don't they realize we are fighting the same type of bid for world takeover here in Viet Nam, as we did against Hitler in Europe, and Japan in the Pacific? The tactics have changed, but the question is the same—are we to have another . . . Pearl Harbor. We can fight the war now and in Viet Nam, or in 10 years in Mexico and South America, and maybe even in our own United States. . . .

Thank you again,

Rick

As the war dragged on and the soldiers' frustrations and bitterness mounted, many grew more tolerant of the peace movement. Infantryman Stephen Pickett wrote in November 1967 that the troops were "well informed here about the demonstrations by both sides. Even though I'm here, I still have an open mind." Infantry Sergeant Joseph Morrissey confided in a letter to his brother in late 1969, "This place is sort of getting to me. I've been seeing too many guys getting messed up. . . . I hope you do protest against war or sing for peace—I would." For Ron Kovic, wounded in combat at age nineteen, the discovery that he would never walk again was "the end of whatever belief I'd still had in what I'd done in Vietnam." Returning home, Kovic took a leading role among the antiwar protesters he had once despised.

JEFF SCHOMP OF LIVINGSTON, NEW JERSEY, WAS DRAFTED IN 1969 AND SERVED IN VIETNAM FOR A YEAR AS AN ARMY INTERPRETER. LIKE MANY OF THE YOUNG MEN DRAFTED IN THE LATER YEARS OF THE WAR, JEFF HAD TAKEN PART IN HOMEFRONT ANTIWAR RALLIES, SIT-INS, AND PETITION DRIVES. HE CHOSE NOT TO AVOID THE DRAFT, HE WROTE, "BECAUSE I LOVE MY COUNTRY, DESPITE ITS FAULTS." IN THIS LETTER TO HIS HOMETOWN NEWSPAPER, JEFF RESPONDED TO AN EARLIER WRITER'S CLAIM THAT AMERICAN TROOPS WERE UNIFORMLY OPPOSED TO THE ANTIWAR PROTESTS. HIS LETTER REFERS TO MORATORIUM AGAINST THE WAR DAY, AN ORGANIZED EVENT ON OCTOBER 15, 1969, THAT BROUGHT OUT HUGE CROWDS OF ANTIWAR DEMONSTRATORS IN CITIES ACROSS THE NATION. JEFF WROTE FROM FORT BLISS, TEXAS, WHERE HE WAS STATIONED, AWAITING ORDERS TO SHIP OUT.

Fort Bliss, Texas
October 30, 1969

Dear sir:

I would like to remind Bernice Slagle (Oct. 16) that not all servicemen are "morally and physically suffering" from peace demonstrations. There are thousands of loyal soldiers who regard this war as a catastrophe for America both at home and abroad, and who demonstrated the depth of their concern by participating in the Moratorium-Day activities at bases from here to Vietnam despite official disapproval and threats of harassment.

At the Vietnamese Language School, Ft. Bliss, Texas, where all soldiers are faced with imminent [coming soon] . . . Vietnam duty, over 50% participated in a variety of Moratorium activities ranging from a prayer vigil to a mess hall boycott. I, for one, was encouraged and uplifted rather than "sickened." Until the President redefines our Vietnam policy and sets a reasonable timetable for American disengagement, such peaceful demonstrations will continue at military installations throughout the world.

We do this because we too "love freedom" and "hate tyranny"—whether in Moscow, Hanoi, Saigon or Washington.

P.F.C. Jeff Schomp

Other signs of the upheavals in American society also made their way to Vietnam. Many soldiers grew their hair longer and wore peace-symbol medals or tattoos. Some began to question authority, even refusing to obey orders that seemed particularly pointless or dangerous. At the base camps rock music played day and night, with some popular songs capturing the sense of alienation and rebellion: "We Gotta Get Out of This Place" (The Animals), "I-Feel-Like-I'm-Fixin'-to-Die Rag" (Country Joe McDonald), "The Unknown Soldier" (The Doors). Creedence Clearwater Revival's "Fortunate Son" pointed out the inequities of the draft:

> Some folks are born made to wave the flag;
> ooh, they're red, white and blue.
> And when the band plays "Hail to the chief,"

they point the cannon right at you.
It ain't me, it ain't me—I ain't no senator's son.
It ain't me, it ain't me—I ain't no fortunate one.

Drug abuse was another sign of the times. Seeking escape from their fear, frustration, and boredom, the troops in Vietnam used even more mind-altering drugs than the rebellious youths back home. An estimated half of all GIs used marijuana, and thousands were addicted to heroin, opium, cocaine, or other substances. Some 20,000 men were hospitalized for drug addiction or infections caused by dirty needles.

Most drug and alcohol use took place in the rear areas. Jeff Schomp, stationed at the main U.S. Army camp at Long Binh, observed that "up to 80% of the detachment smokes [marijuana], and is very open about it. Even the 'straights' are now getting turned on." Marine veteran John Catterson recalled an incident in which one soldier

> brought two cans of beer out into the field, and I thought they were going to lynch the guy. We just didn't drink in the field. Didn't smoke dope in the field. You had to depend on everybody. . . . Nobody needs a guy who's even the slightest bit off, who's not paying attention.

By the late 1960s, under President Richard M. Nixon, the United States was gradually winding down its involvement in Vietnam. Nixon had campaigned in 1968 with a promise "to end the war and win the peace." The tactics he used to pursue that goal, however, only heightened the divisions in American society and the crisis of spirit among U.S. military forces. For many GIs in the final years of the conflict, Vietnam would become what one embittered infantryman termed "a war of survival."

Five

A War for Peace

It was just [about] surviving. Save your friends, you save yourself, and it didn't matter about anything else—the United States, Mom, apple pie, the girl you left behind—all that stuff was just for movies and books. . . . The rest of it was just living from one second to the next and hoping that the seconds added up to minutes and hours and days and months so you could go home.

—MARINE VETERAN RALPH STRANG

Vietnamization

When Richard Nixon was sworn in as president in January 1969, America had been fighting in Vietnam for nearly four years. Nixon was a hard-core anti-Communist, but he was also a shrewd and realistic politician. Although he feared that a Communist victory in Vietnam would weaken world confidence in American leadership, he knew that the divisive war had to end. The new president pledged "to bring the American people together." He would win "peace with honor" through a policy of Vietnamization, gradually withdrawing American troops while building up South Vietnam's military strength so the country could defend itself. At the same time, the United States would intensify the air war and intimidate the Communists through threats of drastic actions, including the possibility of a nuclear attack. The goal of this "war for peace" was to force North Vietnam to agree to a "fair negotiated settlement that would preserve the independence of South Vietnam" and give the struggling democratic nation a chance to survive.

In June 1969 the president announced the first troop withdrawals, bringing home 25,000 men. By the year's end, further withdrawals would reduce the number of Americans in Vietnam to 475,000, the lowest point since 1967. Meanwhile, U.S. aid expanded the South Vietnamese army and equipped it with an arsenal of rifles, artillery, tanks, helicopters, and warplanes. Nixon also ordered the secret

President Richard Nixon pays a visit to combat infantrymen at their base just north of Saigon in July 1969.

bombing of North Vietnamese base camps in Cambodia. Despite these actions, Communist negotiators at peace talks held in Paris in mid-1968 declared that they would sit "until the chairs rot" before agreeing to withdraw from the South. North Vietnam was waging its own war of attrition. All it had to do was keep up the pressure until American public opinion forced President Nixon to give up the fight.

Antiwar activists kept fairly quiet during Nixon's first months in office, waiting to see how the new president's policies worked out. But as it became apparent that peace was still years away, the voices of dissent rang out again, louder than ever. Nixon responded with a counterattack. Denouncing his critics as "irresponsible," he called on the "great silent majority" of patriotic Americans to show their support for their government. Vice President Spiro Agnew followed up with angry attacks on the "criminal misfits" whose "tantrums [were] destroying the fabric of American democracy."

These hard-hitting tactics did not silence the government's critics. Instead, they led to further turmoil by whipping up the divisions between hawks and doves. Increasingly, peace demonstrations ended in violence. The worst incidents occurred in April 1972, after President Nixon announced that he was sending American ground troops into Cambodia to seek and destroy enemy bases. College campuses across the country erupted in loud and angry protests. At Kent State University in Ohio, National Guard troops who had been called in to restore order shot and killed four students. Following that tragic incident, antiwar strikes and riots shut down more than four hundred colleges, and 100,000 demonstrators marched on Washington, D.C.

Nixon had been in office a year and a half. The country he had pledged to unite was more divided than ever, and there was still no end in sight for the war he had promised to end.

Crisis in the Military

The drawn-out schedule of troop withdrawals and the ever-widening dissent at home took a heavy toll on U.S. military forces. By the end of 1970, about 335,000 Americans remained in Vietnam. A year later, there were 157,000. The troops no longer conducted large search-and-destroy sweeps deep in enemy territory.

As the morale of American troops deteriorated in the final years of the war, many GIs still tried to do their best and support their buddies.. This soldier is receiving his third Purple Heart, an award given to servicemen and women wounded in action.

Military leaders had ended that practice in late 1969, after 476 Americans were killed or wounded in a grinding battle on Ap Bia Mountain in South Vietnam, known to GIs as "Hamburger Hill." Since then, U.S. ground troops had waged mainly a defensive war. The men spent most of their time guarding military bases and searching the surrounding villages and jungles for enemy troops and supplies. Growing manpower shortages meant that patrols often went into the field at half their usual strength. And for most soldiers, the knowledge that they were fighting for a lost cause left just one objective: to avoid becoming "the last GI to die in Vietnam."

"I really didn't think about the war—about winning or losing," recalled U.S. Army Special Forces veteran Ivan Delbyk. "I just tried to stay alive." GIs saw no point in getting killed in a war without any real military objectives. They joked that their search-and-destroy missions were actually "search-and-evade" operations, since the patrols generally avoided areas where enemy contact was likely. Marine Lieutenant William Broyles, Jr., described how the men in his unit conducted "phantom patrols," faking the action "on our radios, talking to each other from a few feet away as if we were crossing rivers, climbing hills, taking up new positions. We weren't about to risk our lives."

Some field commanders went along with their troops, leading them with the goal of bringing back as many men as possible alive and well. Officers who remained committed to fighting the war in earnest often found themselves challenged by soldiers who refused to obey combat orders. In extreme cases "over-aggressive" or dangerously incompetent officers were threatened or killed. The murder of an officer by his men was called "fragging," from the weapon most commonly used, a fragmentation grenade. One government study found evidence of at least two hundred fraggings in 1970, double the number that had taken place the year before.

IN THIS LETTER TO A FRIEND BACK HOME, PRIVATE THOMAS KINGSLEY (NICKNAMED TARZAN) DESCRIBED THE BITTERNESS AND OUTRAGE OF SOLDIERS WHO FELT THEY HAD BEEN SENT TO FIGHT A SENSELESS WAR. KINGSLEY WENT TO VIETNAM IN DECEMBER 1970 AND WAS KILLED FOUR MONTHS LATER IN THE ACCIDENTAL EXPLOSION OF AN AMERICAN MINE.

[January 1971]

Dear Bob,
The first month has passed unceremoniously and uneventfully, which doesn't displease me in the least. There have been times, though, when I have been scared to death—a couple of times I thought it was all over. . . .

The first night on guard I almost shot up a firefly, which I thought was a gook [racial slur for a Vietnamese] with a flashlight. The second night I heard someone yelling at me. So I woke up the guys around me and they said it was a frog! Sounded just like a person. . . .

Companies all around us are running into contact, and I firmly believe I will not leave here without being shot or injured first. I hate to say it, but that's how it is; the odds of finding trouble are too great, something's got to happen sometime. . . .

I'm so embittered I don't believe it—but there is nothing you can do. . . . It seems no one gives a damn besides us grunts in the bush. You people in the world don't know what's happening because the Army won't let you know and the goddamn lifers [career officers] in the Army could care less. . . .

There's a bitter hatred between us and the South Viet Nam troops because . . . we do all the goddamn fighting while they sit on their asses all the time. Man, it makes you burn. . . .

And how do you react—how do you blow off steam? A lot of guys grow a hatred for all gooks—that's why we have [atrocities like] My Lai. Others take it out on the Army; in Nam they average two frags a week (fragging is where a man simply pulls the pin on a hand grenade and tosses it at a lifer).

It's bigger than that, though—it's the whole goddamn country—to allow such an atrocity to happen. I suppose because nobody really realizes what's happening here or can't imagine or picture it. I know I couldn't.

But I'll tell you, man, if I ever get back there and hear someone say Viet Nam was worthwhile or it was our obligation—I'll hit him right in the face. . . .

Tarzan

The breakdown of discipline and morale also led to other signs of crisis. Racial incidents between black and white troops and acts of violence against Vietnamese civilians increased sharply. Drug use skyrocketed, along with drug-related crimes ranging from theft to murder. The number of soldiers who deserted more than doubled between 1967 and 1970. Meanwhile, most GIs soldiered on, and the number of American casualties continued to rise. During the Nixon administration, more than 20,000 Americans were killed in Vietnam.

"Our army that now remains in Vietnam is in a state approaching collapse," warned retired U.S. Marine Colonel Robert Heinl in early 1971, "with individual units avoiding or having refused combat, murdering their officers . . . , drug-ridden, and dispirited." One GI summed up the situation more bluntly: "The whole thing stinks."

A Peace Agreement

The first test of President Nixon's Vietnamization policy came in early 1971, when South Vietnamese troops invaded neighboring Laos. Their objective was to cut the flow of war supplies down the long portion of the Ho Chi Minh Trail that snaked through that country. The assault was a disaster. When the Communists counter-attacked, the Southern troops withdrew in panic. Only heavy U.S. air support prevented their complete annihilation.

Henry Kissinger signs the Paris peace agreement ending the U.S. war in Vietnam, January 27, 1973. Kissinger was national security adviser to President Nixon and, later, U.S. secretary of state.

A year later, on March 30, 1972, the North Vietnamese launched the Easter Offensive, their largest attack yet against South Vietnam. Many Southern troops fought courageously, but again massive American firepower was needed to beat back the Communists. The South Vietnamese army had nearly a million troops armed with billions of dollars' worth of sophisticated weaponry. Still, it lacked the training, experience, and leadership to succeed on its own.

By this time, only about 65,000 American troops remained in Vietnam. The peace talks had been sputtering along off and on for nearly four years. One of the main obstacles to an agreement was North Vietnam's refusal to withdraw its forces from the South. Under increasing pressure from Congress and the American peo-

Prisoners of War

No one awaited the end of the Vietnam War more eagerly than American prisoners of war and their families. About seven hundred Americans, mostly air force and navy pilots shot down in action, were held as prisoners by the North Vietnamese. Most lived in prison camps in or near Hanoi, where they were subjected to unbelievable brutality.

At the most infamous prison, known as the "Hanoi Hilton," POWs were kept in solitary confinement in seven-foot-square cells crawling with cockroaches and rats. Their meals consisted mainly of watery soup and rice. They were systematically tortured—burned with cigarettes, beaten with rubber hoses, tied with ropes that were tightened to pull their arms and legs out of the sockets. The purpose of the torture was to force the Americans to "confess" to their "war crimes." Many endured months of savage treatment before cooperating. In 1966, after prolonged torture, navy pilot Jeremiah Denton agreed to appear in a televised press conference to publicize U.S. "war atrocities." During the interview, Denton blinked his eyes in Morse code, repeatedly spelling out the message "T-O-R-T-U-R-E."

ple to end the war, Nixon and his chief negotiator, national security adviser Henry Kissinger, finally dropped that demand. In January 1973 the two sides reached a settlement.

The Paris Peace Accords called for a cease-fire, the withdrawal of all remaining U.S. forces, and the release of all American prisoners of war. Like the settlement that had ended the French war two decades earlier, however, the accords left Vietnam's political future undecided. For the time being, North and South Vietnam would each hold on to the lands they occupied, and Nguyen Van Thieu (nyen-vahn-TYOO), who had been elected South Vietnam's president in late 1967, would remain in power. Sometime in the future an international commission would be set

Such acts of defiance helped POWs hold on to their dignity and survive their ordeal. The men encouraged one another by communicating through codes tapped on the walls and floors. One code used a twenty-five-letter alphabet (with C doubling for K), arranged this way:

A	B	C	D	E
F	G	H	I	J
L	M	N	O	P
Q	R	S	T	U
V	W	X	Y	Z

The first tap indicated the row number of a letter, the second tap its column number. A prisoner returning from a torture session knew that his fellow captives were pulling for him when he heard this: •• •• (two taps, two taps, for G), • •• (B), •••• ••••• (U). "GBU" was short for "God Bless You."

After the Paris Peace Accords were signed, North Vietnam began releasing the POWs. By April 1973, 591 American prisoners had returned home. Dozens more are believed to have died in captivity, some from outright murder, some from abuse and inadequate food and medical care.

SERVICEMEN AND WOMEN RETURNING HOME FROM VIETNAM OFTEN FELT A BEWILDERING TANGLE OF EMOTIONS: JOY, RELIEF, ANTICIPATION, ANXIETY, GUILT OVER THE BUDDIES LEFT BEHIND. INFANTRY SERGEANT JOHN "BUTCH" HAGMANN SERVED TWO TOURS IN VIETNAM, IN 1965 AND FROM JULY 1966 TO JULY 1967. SHORTLY BEFORE HIS SECOND HOMECOMING, HE SHARED HIS FEELINGS IN THIS LETTER TO HIS PARENTS.

24 May 67

Dear Mom & Dad,

. . . It sure is going to be different being around clean things again. I hope I can take it. It's going to take a while to get used to stateside living. Guess I'll have to watch my manners.

You know, when you get over here all you think about is getting back to the World. But when your time gets near, it sort of scares you because you know in your heart that you're not like the people back home. It's a funny feeling to be afraid to go home, but everyone over here feels the same. . . . There are a lot of mixed emotions—worrying about hurting the people close to you, or maybe your dreams about the States will shatter when you get home. And then there's always the way you regret leaving your buddies in this hell hole. We all joke about "Put your time in," but in our hearts we wish we could all go home together. . . .

All my love,
Butch

The Fall of Saigon

The Paris peace agreement ended U.S. involvement in Vietnam, but it did not end the war. Even as the cease-fire officially took effect on January 27, 1973, fighting continued all across South Vietnam. Without U.S. support the Southern forces steadily lost ground.

President Nixon had promised "swift and severe retaliatory action" if the Communists violated the agreement. By mid-1973, however, the president's public approval ratings and political power were at an all-time low. Nixon was battling charges related to his role in the political scandal known as the Watergate affair. On August 9, 1974, facing the threat of impeachment, he resigned from office. Vice President Gerald Ford succeeded him. Burdened by domestic problems and a defiant Congress determined to end America's "endless support for an endless war," President Ford made only a halfhearted effort to save South Vietnam.

By late April 1975, only about one thousand Americans remained in Saigon. These included U.S. Embassy officials and guards, businesspeople, journalists, and charity workers. On April 29 they heard a bizarre broadcast over the U.S.-owned radio station: the song "White Christmas" playing over and over again. It was a prearranged signal. The North Vietnamese were closing in on the capital and Americans should head for evacuation points on the rooftops of the embassy and other Saigon buildings. Scenes of panic and chaos followed, with both Americans and South Vietnamese fighting their way through the crowded streets, hoping to board the helicopters shuttling between the city and U.S. Navy ships anchored offshore.

OPERATION FREQUENT WIND—THE FINAL U.S. EVACUATION FROM VIETNAM—BEGAN ON APRIL 29, 1975. U.S. NAVY CAPTAIN R. E. KEMBLE WAS MASTER OF ONE OF THE EVACUATION SHIPS ANCHORED OFF SAIGON. IN HIS OFFICIAL REPORT ON THE OPERATION, KEMBLE DESCRIBED THE CHAOTIC SCENE AS TENS OF THOUSANDS OF DESPERATE SOUTH VIETNAMESE WHO COULD NOT REACH THE RESCUE HELICOPTERS SOUGHT ESCAPE BY BOAT.

On the 29th at 0700 hours it appeared as if an attack on Vung Tau [southeast of Saigon] was in progress. Large splashes observed in the water along shore and several explosions observed on shore in the resort section of the city. Many rounds heard going off in the distance inland and several areas of the city were completely obscured with smoke. Started loading refugees in increasing numbers. As the refugees would come aboard they would abandon their boats and let them drift off. Enemy action still going strong at Vung Tau so for the safety of all concerned, anchorage was shifted to 6 miles off of Vung Tau. We towed four fishing boats out with us and many more followed under their own power.

At the anchorage loading commenced immediately with all hands including security personnel now engaged in loading refugees. Accommodation ladders, pilot ladders and cargo nets being used to load refugees. Security personnel were screening the refugees as they came aboard and confiscating weapons. By 1600 a continuous stream of vessels and anything else that would float were alongside the vessel and the crew loading them as fast as possible. At 1720 stopped loading refugees upon orders not to exceed 6000. Had to cut boats loose and steam. . . .

At 1745 received orders . . . to continue loading and to take up to 8000 refugees. Stopped the ship and shortly the boats that were following us caught up and we commenced embarking more refugees. At 1900 received orders from Saigon to load up to 10,000 refugees. At that time at least 80 boats were moored or milling alongside with hundreds streaming towards us. Refugees almost in panic stage trying to get on board. Loading refugees by cargo booms, ladders and nets. The sight was unbelievable. . . . At least 20 or more refugees in each cargo net . . . including women . . . with small babies in their arms hanging on to cargo nets with small children hanging on to their mothers—and still they come. The situation was pitiful, unbelievable and heart rending. No assistance from other ships received. At 2000 hours we had to stop with an estimated 10,000 refugees on board and just no room for any others. 70 or 80 boats were still alongside and pleading with us to please take them and more boats still observed coming towards us. We had to cut boats loose in order to get away. It's a sight that will be impressed in everyone's memory for a long time. We did our best and yet it seemed so inadequate.

Just before eight o'clock the next morning, the last helicopter lifted off from the roof of the U.S. Embassy. All the Americans had been evacuated, but thousands of desperate Vietnamese who had worked for the U.S. government were left behind. A few hours later, tanks crashed through the gates of the Presidential Palace. North Vietnamese soldiers triumphantly raised their flag over the capital, renaming it Ho Chi Minh City.

"South Vietnam had fallen," said Stephen Klinkhammer, a navy medic aboard one of the evacuation ships.

South Vietnamese refugees escape advancing Communist forces during the fall of Saigon, April 1975.

You could see the explosions from the sea. . . . There were people coming out in boats, half-sinking boats. . . . The flight deck
was so full of choppers [helicopters] that we had to push them
overboard because there was no room. . . . We ended up with
three thousand civilians aboard. . . . That was the best we could
do. . . . I still . . . wake up with bad dreams that I have of taking
fire and watching people being murdered and being a part of the
process. . . . I have cried my ass off. I don't have any tears left.

Conclusion

Veterans' Voices

More than 58,000 American servicemen and women died in the Vietnam War. Another 300,000 were wounded, including nearly 100,000 with severe disabilities such as blindness or amputated limbs. About 2,000 GIs are still listed as missing in action.

An unknown number of veterans suffer from physical and psychological problems related to their service. These include nearly 100,000 with a variety of illnesses, from skin rashes to cancer, that may have resulted from exposure to herbicides such as Agent Orange, which were used to kill jungle growth and deny cover to enemy forces in Vietnam.

Those are the numbers. They only hint at the impact Vietnam had on the Americans who worked and fought there. Some veterans were never able to put their feelings of anger, pain, guilt, and loss behind them. The majority readjusted well to civilian life, settling down, finding jobs, raising families. But no one came home from service in Vietnam untouched or unchanged. For a sense of the many ways veterans have looked back on their experiences, we conclude by listening to the voices of a few who served.

Walter McIntosh, U.S. Army intelligence specialist and CIA operative, 1965–1975
"I was in Vietnam for a very long time, got shot once, was injured a bit more seriously by an errant water buffalo, but I survived. . . . I still feel a very real commitment to the Vietnamese people who were promised at least a chance to earn a life

Service in Vietnam left many veterans with lasting physical and emotional scars. "Life goes on—mostly good, sometimes bad," said one veteran after the war, "and there seems to be a hole where part of my heart used to be."

that included freedom from the enslavement of communism and a hope for a future for their children."

Ken Moorefield, U.S. State Department foreign service officer, 1967–1975
"I'm sure that Vietnam will always live within me. And I don't want it not to be there. Vietnam veterans experienced something that transcended ourselves. Despite the fact that we suffered a political defeat, the values for which we fought are larger than each of us."

Elizabeth Allen, U.S. Army nurse, 1967–1968
"What this country owes [women veterans], if 'owe' is the word, is the same as we give any warrior. And that every time we sing 'The Star-Spangled Banner' . . . and we really get off on 'the rockets red glare, bombs bursting in air, gave proof through the night that our flag is still there'—that there are soldiers, both men and women, that have given that assurance, and you 'owe' for that assurance. And if you don't want to pay it, don't sing the song."

William Ehrhart, U.S. Marines, 1967–1968
"I don't have nightmares about killing armed soldiers in combat. The thing I have nightmares about is the woman in the rice field that I shot one day because she was running—for no other reason—because she was running away from the Americans who were going to kill her, and I killed her. Fifty-five, 60 years old, unarmed. And at the time I didn't even think twice about it."

Vietnam veteran Scott Brooks-Miller
"Yes, I'm bitter, and probably always will be. We were not politicians—most of us couldn't even vote. We simply did what we were asked to do, just as our fathers and grandfathers and all the generations preceding did. But because it was an unpopular war, we took the brunt of the anger of the American people."

Joe McDonald, singer, songwriter, and U.S. Navy veteran, 1959–1962
"Because we paid, and are still paying, such a dear price, it is hard to forgive and forget. The country used and abused and then attempted to disown and discredit the Vietnam War generation. And let that be the lesson for the younger generations, so that it was not all in vain. Everyone has a right to be treated fairly and honestly. And a right to question authority. You have a right to live."

From a note left at the Vietnam Veterans Memorial in Washington, D.C.
"This wedding ring belonged to a young Viet Cong fighter. He was killed by a Marine unit in the Phu Loc province of South Vietnam in May of 1968. I wish I knew more about this young man. I have carried this ring for 18 years and it's time for me to lay it down. This boy is not my enemy any longer."

Time Line of Vietnam War Events

1945	1946	1954	1955
SEPTEMBER 2 Ho Chi Minh proclaims Vietnam's independence from Japanese occupation and French rule.	**DECEMBER 20** The French Indochina War begins.	**MAY 7** Ho Chi Minh's guerrillas defeat the French at Dien Bien Phu. **JULY 21** The Geneva Accords divide Vietnam along the 17th parallel, with the Communists ruling in the North and a non-Communist Vietnamese government in the South.	**FEBRUARY 12** The United States sends advisers to train the South Vietnamese army. **OCTOBER 26** U.S.-backed Ngo Dinh Diem becomes president of South Vietnam.

1959	1960	1963	1964
APRIL 4 President Dwight Eisenhower pledges to maintain South Vietnam as a separate state.	NOVEMBER 8 John F. Kennedy is elected 35th president of the United States. DECEMBER 20 North Vietnamese Communist leaders form the National Liberation Front to overthrow the government of South Vietnam.	NOVEMBER 1 A military coup overthrows the Diem government. NOVEMBER 22 President Kennedy is assassinated; Vice President Lyndon Johnson becomes president. NOVEMBER 23 President Johnson announces continued U.S. support for South Vietnam.	AUGUST 7 Congress passes the Tonkin Gulf Resolution, giving the president unlimited power to resist aggression in Southeast Asia. NOVEMBER 3 Lyndon Johnson is elected president.

1973	1974	1975	
JANUARY 27 The United States, North Vietnam, South Vietnam, and the Vietcong sign the Paris Peace Accords, agreeing to a cease-fire and withdrawal of U.S. troops from Vietnam. **MARCH 29** The last U.S. combat troops leave Vietnam.	**AUGUST 9** Nixon resigns to avoid impeachment for his role in the Watergate scandal; Vice President Gerald Ford becomes president.	**APRIL 30** Saigon surrenders to North Vietnam.	

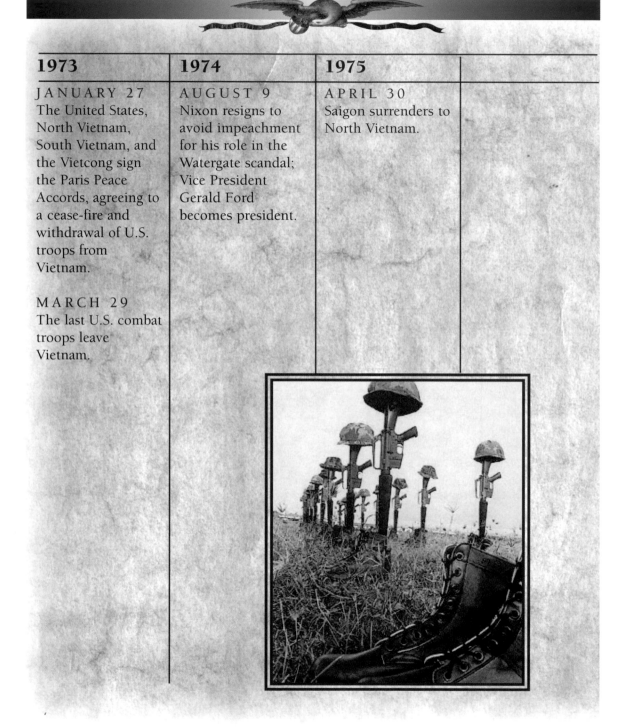

Glossary

Airmobile Division A U.S. Army division in Vietnam that relied on helicopters for transporting soldiers to the battlefield and providing fire support during assaults.

Black Panthers Members of a militant black movement organized in the mid-1960s to fight for liberation from white oppression.

Cold War The period between the end of World War II in 1945 and the collapse of the Soviet Union in the early 1990s, marked by hostility between the democratic nations of the West and the Soviet Union and other Communist nations.

Communism A system in which all property is owned and controlled by the government and is supposed to be shared equally by all citizens.

detachment A small military unit permanently assigned to special duties.

domino theory An idea often used to justify U.S. intervention in Vietnam, which held that if one of the nations of Southeast Asia fell to Communist power, the rest would topple like a row of dominoes. Debate over the theory still continues: after the Vietnam War, Cambodia and Laos were taken over by the Communists, but the other "dominoes" did not fall; supporters of the theory argue that this was because the U.S. involvement gave the nations of the region time to strengthen their defenses against aggression.

draft cards Identification cards issued to men who were eligible for the draft.

FAC (forward air controller) A pilot who flew in a slow, low-flying plane over bombing targets in Vietnam, while radioing information to fighter and bomber pilots about the target and the location of troops and civilians on the ground.

firefight A brief but fierce exchange of fire between enemies.

fragging The murder of an unpopular military officer by his own men, often by a fragmentation grenade, which breaks into many small fragments upon explosion and leaves no fingerprints.

GI A member of the U.S. armed forces; the term comes from the soldiers' "government issue" supplies.

guerrilla (pronounced like "gorilla") A type of fighting or fighter that uses surprise and stealth instead of direct combat to wear down a better-equipped enemy.

herbicides Chemicals used to kill plants or strip their leaves.

infantry The foot soldiers of an army.

nationalist A person dedicated to a nation's independence.

point man The forward man on a combat patrol.

propaganda Ideas or information, often untrue or misleading, spread by a government or an organization to influence public opinion.

satchel charges Packs containing explosives.

siege A blockade of an enemy position, in which the attackers cut off food and other supplies to force a surrender.

Special Forces U.S. Army troops who conduct special operations such as intelligence gathering and antiguerrilla training behind enemy lines.

stand-down A state of rest and relaxation between military missions.

teach-ins Mass meetings on college campuses, in which students and teachers discussed the war.

Vietcong Vietnamese guerrillas who fought for the overthrow of the South Vietnamese government and were largely directed and supported by the Communist government of North Vietnam; also called VC, Charlie, or Victor.

Watergate A political scandal involving abuses of power during President Richard Nixon's administration, which led to his resignation in August 1974. Nixon authorized illegal activities to gather information on his opponents, including a break-in at Democratic Party headquarters in the Watergate building in Washington, D.C., as well as a government cover-up of the crimes.

To Find Out More

BOOKS

Dudley, William, ed. *The Vietnam War.* Opposing Viewpoints series. San Diego, CA: Greenhaven Press, 1998.

Primary sources are used to illustrate a variety of opinions on issues surrounding the Vietnam War, including the commitment of U.S. combat troops, the effectiveness of Vietnamization, and the impact of media coverage on American public opinion.

Edmonds, Anthony O. *The War in Vietnam.* Historic Events of the Twentieth Century series. Westport, CT: Greenwood Press, 1998.
Designed for high school and college students, this analysis of the causes and events of the war includes biographies of key figures, historical documents, a time line, and a glossary.

Gay, Kathlyn, and Martin Gay. *Vietnam War.* Voices from the Past series. New York: Henry Holt, 1996.
Reflections by Americans who lived through the Vietnam years, both on the battlefront and the homefront, bring a personal view to this easy-to-read account of the war.

Hoobler, Dorothy, and Thomas Hoobler. *Vietnam: Why We Fought*. New York: Knopf, 1990.
This illustrated history offers an objective look at the major events of the war.

Schomp, Virginia. *The Vietnam War*. New York: Benchmark Books, 2002.
Companion title in the Letters from the Homefront series.

Summers, Harry G., Jr. *Vietnam War Almanac*. New York: Facts on File, 1985.
This comprehensive reference book includes alphabetically arranged articles on about five hundred war-related topics, plus maps, photographs, and a detailed time line.

Wright, David. *Causes and Consequences of the Vietnam War*. Austin, TX: Raintree Steck-Vaughn, 1996.
Illustrated with a number of photographs and maps, this book examines the history of Vietnam, events in the French and American wars, and the legacy of U.S. involvement in Southeast Asia.

Zeinert, Karen. *The Valiant Women of the Vietnam War*. Brookfield, CT: Millbrook Press, 2000.
This is a well-written examination of the roles American women played in Vietnam as civilian volunteers and in the armed forces.

VIDEOS

Vietnam: A Television History. Written by Andrew Pearson. Produced by WGBH Educational Foundation, Boston, 1983. Distributed by Sony Video Software Company.
This seven-volume video series won six Emmy Awards for its detailed visual and oral accounts of the history, costs, and consequences of the Vietnam War. Contains some graphic images and descriptions of war's violence.

Vietnam: The Ten Thousand Day War. Written by Peter Arnett. Distributed by Bonneville Worldwide Entertainment, Salt Lake City, Utah, 1998.

Stunning live-action footage brings alive the American experience in Vietnam from 1945 through 1975.

ON THE INTERNET*

"Go Places with TFK: Vietnam" from Time for Kids Online, © 2000 Time Inc., at
   http://www.timeforkids.com/TFK/specials/articles/0,6709,187312,00.html
This is a colorful site offering a virtual tour of famous places in Vietnam, a time line of events throughout the country's history, and a look at a day in the life of a Vietnamese child. Click on "Native Lingo" to hear useful phrases such as "The dog ate my homework" spoken in Vietnamese.

"Investigating the Vietnam War" at http://www.spartacus.schoolnet.co.uk/vietnam.
   html
Designed to help students conduct research into the Vietnam War, this website offers links to Internet sources on a wide variety of topics, including background information, personal narratives, statistics, and visual images. You can also conduct e-mail interviews with a number of veterans and other people who were involved in the war.

"New Jersey Vietnam Veterans' Memorial Foundation" at http://www.njvvmf.org
The website of the New Jersey Vietnam Veterans' Memorial and Vietnam Era Educational Center includes photographs and a virtual tour of the center's facilities, as well as links to other memorials, museums, and information sources.

"Vietnam Online," produced by The American Experience and WGBH Interactive,
   with assistance from PBS Online, at http://www.pbs.org/wgbh/amex/vietnam
Developed to accompany the television series Vietnam: A Television History, *this site offers biographies, U.S. government documents, photos, maps, a glossary, a time line, and articles on weapons, aircraft, POWs and MIAs, and the My Lai Massacre.*

*Websites change from time to time. For additional on-line information, check with the media specialist at your local library.

"Vietnam Veterans Memorial" at http://www.nps.gov/vive/memorial/memorial.htm
This National Park Service website provides photos and information related to the Vietnam Veterans Memorial in Washington, D.C., including the Wall, the Three Servicemen Statue, and the Vietnam Women's Memorial.

"The Vietnam War" at http://www.vietnampix.com/index.html
Stunning photos of soldiers from both sides, most taken by combat photographer Tim Page, are accompanied by a concise history of U.S. involvement in Vietnam. Click on "Site Map" to see all the images at once.

Bibliography

Boettcher, Thomas D. *Vietnam: The Valor and the Sorrow.* Boston: Little, Brown, 1985.

Carroll, Andrew, ed. *War Letters: Extraordinary Correspondence from American Wars.* New York: Scribner, 2001.

Denenberg, Barry. *Voices from Vietnam.* New York: Scholastic, 1995.

Dougan, Clark, Samuel Lipsman, and the editors of Boston Publishing Company. *A Nation Divided.* Boston: Boston Publishing Company, 1984.

Dougan, Clark, Stephen Weiss, and the editors of Boston Publishing Company. *The American Experience in Vietnam.* Boston: Boston Publishing, 1988.

Dudley, William, ed. *The Vietnam War.* San Diego, CA: Greenhaven Press, 1998.

Edelman, Bernard, ed. *Dear America: Letters Home from Vietnam.* New York: Pocket Books, 1985.

Edmonds, Anthony O. *The War in Vietnam.* Westport, CT: Greenwood Press, 1998.

Hardy, Gordon, and the editors of Boston Publishing Company. *Words of War: An Anthology of Vietnam War Literature.* Boston: Boston Publishing Company, 1988.

Herring, George C. *America's Longest War: The United States and Vietnam, 1950–1975.* Philadelphia: Temple University Press, 1986.

Goff, Stanley, Robert Sanders, and Clark Smith. *Brothers: Black Soldiers in the Nam.* Novato, CA: Presidio, 1982.

Greene, Bob. *Homecoming: When the Soldiers Returned from Vietnam.* New York: G. P. Putnam's, 1989.

Hoobler, Dorothy, and Thomas Hoobler. *Vietnam: Why We Fought.* New York: Knopf, 1990.

John F. Kennedy inaugural address, January 20, 1961, History and Politics Out Loud, ©1999–2000 Jerry Goldman and Northwestern University, at http://database.library.northwestern.edu/hpol/transcript.asp?id=10

Karnow, Stanley. *Vietnam: A History.* New York: Penguin, 1984.

Kovic, Ron. *Born on the Fourth of July.* New York: McGraw-Hill, 1976.

The Long Way Home Project at http://www.longwayhome.net

Maclear, Michael. *The Ten Thousand Day War: Vietnam, 1945–1975.* New York: St. Martin's Press, 1981.

McCloud, Bill. *What Should We Tell Our Children about Vietnam?* Norman, OK: University of Oklahoma Press, 1989.

Marks, Richard E. *The Letters of Pfc. Richard E. Marks, USMC.* Philadelphia: J. B. Lippincott, 1967.

Marrin, Albert. *America and Vietnam: The Elephant and the Tiger.* New York: Viking, 1992.

Marshall, Kathryn. *In the Combat Zone: An Oral History of American Women in Vietnam.* Boston: Little, Brown, 1987.

Maurer, Harry. *Strange Ground: Americans in Vietnam, 1945–1975, An Oral History.* New York: Henry Holt, 1989.

Oberdorfer, Don. *Tet!* New York: Da Capo Press, 1984.

O'Nan, Stewart, ed. *The Vietnam Reader.* New York: Doubleday, 1998.

Palmer, Laura. *Shrapnel in the Heart: Letters and Remembrances from the Vietnam Veterans Memorial.* New York: Random House, 1987.

The Pentagon Papers as Published by the New York Times. New York: Quadrangle, 1971.

Pratt, John Clark, ed. *Vietnam Voices: Perspectives on the War Years, 1941–1982.* New York: Penguin, 1984.

Santoli, Al. *Everything We Had: An Oral History of the Vietnam War by Thirty-three American Soldiers Who Fought It.* New York: Random House, 1981.

———. *To Bear Any Burden: The Vietnam War and Its Aftermath in the Words of Americans and Southeast Asians.* New York: Dutton, 1985.

Summers, Harry G., Jr. *Vietnam War Almanac.* New York: Facts on File, 1985.

Terry, Wallace. *Bloods: An Oral History of the Vietnam War by Black Veterans.* New York: Random House, 1984.

Tucker, Spencer C., ed. *The Encyclopedia of the Vietnam War: A Political, Social, & Military History.* New York: Oxford University Press, 1998.

Van Devanter, Lynda. *Home before Morning: The Story of an Army Nurse in Vietnam.* New York: Warner Books, 1983.

Vietnam: Women at War, Discovery Online, Discovery Communications, Inc., at http://tlc.discovery.com/tlcpages/vietnam/stories.html

Walker, Keith. *A Piece of My Heart: The Stories of Twenty-six American Women Who Served in Vietnam.* Novato, CA: Presidio Press, 1985.

Williams, William Appleman, Thomas McCormick, Lloyd Gardner, and Walter LaFeber, eds. *America in Vietnam: A Documentary History.* Garden City, NY: Doubleday, 1985.

Wright, David. *Causes and Consequences of the Vietnam War.* Austin, TX: Raintree Steck-Vaughn, 1996.

Notes on Quotes

The quotations in this book are from the following sources:

Introduction: Tracing the Roots
p. 5, "We hold the truth": Karnow, *Vietnam*, p. 135.
p. 7, *"la sale guerre"*: ibid., p. 188.

Chapter One: America Makes a Commitment
p. 9, "You have a row": Williams and others, *America in Vietnam*, p. 156.
p. 9, "all available means": Herring, *America's Longest War*, p. 44.
p. 10, "Our idea in Vietnam": Maurer, *Strange Ground*, pp. 85, 89.
p. 11, "miracle man": Herring, *America's Longest War*, p. 66.
p. 12, "Although he professes": *Pentagon Papers*, p. 73.
p. 12, "serious danger": Herring, *America's Longest War*, p. 70.
p. 13, "pay any price": *John F. Kennedy inaugural address, History and Politics Out Loud.*
p. 13, "red tide": Herring, *America's Longest War*, p. 43.
p. 13, "in its hour": *John F. Kennedy inaugural address, History and Politics Out Loud.*
p. 13, "The troops": Denenberg, *Voices from Vietnam*, p. 15.
p. 15, "that bitch of a war": Maclear, *Ten Thousand Day War*, p. 83.
p. 16, "bolder actions": Dougan and Weiss, *American Experience in Vietnam*, p. 22.
p. 16, "to take all": Edmonds, *War in Vietnam*, p. 138.
p. 16, "the nose": Hoobler and Hoobler, *Vietnam*, p. 76.
p. 16, "change of mission": *Pentagon Papers*, p. 452.

Chapter Two: Into the Tunnel

p. 19, "It's not like": *Vietnam: A Television History,* Episode 5: *America Takes Charge, 1965–1967.*

p. 19, "gung ho": Santoli, *To Bear Any Burden,* pp. 105–106.

p. 19, "didn't know much": McCloud, *What Should We Tell Our Children,* p. 73.

p. 21, "The way we move": Edelman, *Dear America,* p. 57.

p. 22, "We live in mud": ibid., pp. 60–61.

p. 23, "It was better": Karnow, *Vietnam,* p. 470.

p. 24, "They all looked alike": ibid., p. 467.

p. 25, "winning the hearts": Tucker, *Encyclopedia of the Vietnam War,* p. 73.

p. 25, "a Vietnamese woman": Greene, *Homecoming,* p. 119.

p. 26, "herded like cattle": Karnow, *Vietnam,* pp. 467–468.

p. 28, "We'd take [a] territory": Denenberg, *Voices from Vietnam,* p. 97.

p. 28, "Chasing a VC": Santoli, *To Bear Any Burden,* p. 109.

p. 29, "It began to seem": Karnow, *Vietnam,* p. 472.

p. 29, "Under the Rules": Santoli, *To Bear Any Burden,* p. 142.

p. 29, "sites that they": ibid., p. 144.

p. 29, "never one time": Maurer, *Strange Ground,* p. 387.

p. 31, "We are not going": Dougan and Weiss, *American Experience,* p. 116.

p. 32, "in a face-to-face": Karnow, *Vietnam,* p. 533.

p. 32, "the light": Dougan and Weiss, *American Experience,* p. 152.

p. 33, "the first in": ibid., p. 161.

Chapter Three: Minorities and Women in the War

p. 34, "The government": Goff and others, *Brothers,* pp. 29–30.

p. 34, "In Vietnam": Terry, *Bloods,* p. xvi.

pp. 34–35, "A few of us": ibid., p. 219.

p. 36, "a white man's war": Goff and others, *Brothers,* p. ix.

p. 38, "A barrier": Santoli, *To Bear Any Burden,* p. 191.

p. 38, "When I heard": Terry, *Bloods,* p. 172.

p. 38, "This infantry unit": Maurer, *Strange Ground,* p. 241.

p. 39, "It wasn't only": ibid., pp. 172, 173, 178.

p. 40, "Never before": Goff and others, *Brothers,* pp. x, xi.

p. 40, "Not even working": Marshall, *In the Combat Zone,* p. 29.

p. 41, "He lost both legs": ibid., p. 86.

p. 42, "a total emotional": ibid., p. 56.

p. 42, "ghosts": Van Devanter, *Home Before Morning,* pp. 356, 361.

p. 42, "the war was wrong": Marshall, *In the Combat Zone,* pp. 86, 89, 90, 91.

Chapter Four: Questions and Confrontations

p. 43, "I was in Vietnam": Kovic, *Born on the Fourth of July*, p. 119.

p. 45, "a national disgrace": Summers, *Vietnam Almanac*, p. 146.

p. 46, "very difficult": Dougan and others, *A Nation Divided*, p. 158.

p. 47, "people opposing": Marks, *Letters*, pp. 96–97.

p. 47, "the hippies": Kovic, *Born on the Fourth of July*, p. 119.

p. 48, "well informed": Edelman, *Dear America*, p. 212.

p. 48, "This place": ibid., p. 223.

p. 48, "the end of whatever": Kovic, *Born on the Fourth of July*, p. 119.

p. 48, "Because I love": "To the Editor," Livingston, New Jersey, *West Essex Tribune*, June 5, 1969.

pp. 49–50, "Some folks are born": O'Nan, *Vietnam Reader*, p. 288.

p. 50, "up to 80%": Schomp, Jeff, "Vietnam Journal," November 12, 1970.

p. 50, "brought two cans": Maurer, *Strange Ground*, p. 199.

p. 50, "to end the war": Dougan and Weiss, *American Experience in Vietnam*, p. 229.

p. 50, "a war of survival": Edelman, *Dear America*, p. 216.

Chapter Five: A War for Peace

p. 51, "It was just": Edmonds, *War in Vietnam*, p. 151.

p. 51, "to bring the American": Dougan, *Nation Divided*, p. 146.

p. 51, "peace with honor": Herring, *America's Longest War*, p. 221.

p. 52, "war for peace": ibid., p. 223.

p. 52, "fair negotiated settlement": ibid., p. 224.

p. 53, "until the chairs rot": ibid., p. 226.

p. 53, "irresponsible" and "great silent majority": Dougan and Weiss, *American Experience in Vietnam*, p. 242.

p. 53, "criminal misfits": Dudley, *Vietnam War*, p. 223.

p. 53, "tantrums [were] destroying": Hardy, *Words of War*, p. 167.

p. 54, "the last GI": Maurer, *Strange Ground*, p. 505.

p. 54, "I really didn't": Maclear, *Ten Thousand Day War*, p. 277.

p. 54, "on our radios": Boettcher, *Vietnam*, p. 399.

p. 56, "Our army": ibid.

p. 56, "the whole thing": Marrin, *America and Vietnam*, p. 220.

p. 60, "We have finally": Karnow, *Vietnam*, p. 654.

p. 60, "One day": McCloud, *What Should We Tell Our Children*, p. 7.

p. 60, "a year of unbelievable": Greene, *Homecoming*, p. 20.

p. 60, "not a very good": ibid., pp. 52–53.

p. 62, "swift and severe": Karnow, *Vietnam*, p. 651.

p. 63, "endless support": Herring, *America's Longest War*, p. 263.

pp. 64, 66, "South Vietnam": Santoli, *Everything We Had*, pp. 252, 254, 255.

Conclusion: Veterans' Voices

p. 68, "I was in Vietnam": Edmonds, *War in Vietnam,* p. 163.

p. 68, "I'm sure": Santoli, *To Bear Any Burden,* p. 335.

p. 69, "What this country": *Vietnam: Women at War.*

p. 69, "I don't have": Denenberg, *Voices from Vietnam,* p. 86.

p. 69, "Yes, I'm bitter": Greene, *Homecoming,* p. 18.

p. 69, "Because we paid": McCloud, *What Should We Tell Our Children,* p. 85.

p. 69, "This wedding ring": Palmer, *Shrapnel in the Heart,* p. 184.

Acknowledgments

Every effort has been made to trace the copyright holders of the letters reprinted in this book. We apologize for any omissions or errors in this regard and would be pleased to make the appropriate acknowledgments in any future printings.

Grateful acknowledgments are made to the following historical societies, libraries, publishers, and individuals:

John F. Kennedy to Bobbie Lou Pendergrass, March 6, 1963. White House Central Subject File, Box 604, John Fitzgerald Kennedy Library, Boston, MA. Courtesy of the National Archives and Records Administration.

George Ball to Lyndon B. Johnson, July 1, 1965. From *The Pentagon Papers: The Defense Department History of United States Decisionmaking on Vietnam, the Senator Gravel Edition,* Vol. 4, Boston: Beacon Press, 1975.

Frank McCarthy narrative. From Santoli, Al, *To Bear Any Burden: The Vietnam War and Its Aftermath in the Words of Americans and Southeast Asians,* New York: Dutton, 1985. Reprinted by permission of the author.

Robert A. Tillquist, November 2, 1965. Reprinted by permission of Jean Risley.

"Guerrilla War" is reprinted from *Beautiful Wreckage: New & Selected Poems by W. D. Ehrhart,* Easthampton, MA: Adastra Press, 1999, by permission of the author.

Robert Kirk narrative. From *Vietnam: The Heartland Remembers* by Stanley W. Beesley. Copyright © 1987 by the University of Oklahoma Press. Reprinted by permission of the publisher.

Richard Ford narrative. From *Bloods: An Oral History of the Vietnam War by Black Veterans* by Wallace Terry, copyright © 1984 by Wallace Terry. Used by permission of Arlington House, a division of Random House, Inc.

Lynda Van Devanter to her parents. From Van Devanter, Lynda, *Home Before Morning: The Story of an Army Nurse in Vietnam,* New York: Warner Books, 1983.

Richard E. Marks to Mr. Peter Whiting, July 7, 1965. From *The Letters of Pfc. Richard E. Marks, USMC* by Richard E. Marks, copyright © 1987 by Gloria D. Kramer, executrix of the Estate of Richard E. Marks. Reprinted by permission of HarperCollins Publishers, Inc.

Jeff Schomp to the Livingston, New Jersey, *West Essex Tribune,* October 30, 1969. Author's personal collection.

Thomas Kingsley to Bob, January 1971. From *Harper's* 248 (June 1974).

John "Butch" Hagmann to his parents, May 24, 1967. Originally appeared in *Dear America: Letters Home from Vietnam,* edited by Bernard Edelman for the New York Vietnam Veterans Memorial Commission. Published by W. W. Norton & Company, 1985, 2002. Reprinted by permission of Bernard Edelman.

R. E. Kemble narrative. From Captain (U.S.N.) R. E. Kemble, Report to Commander, Subject: "Vietnam Sealift Evacuation History," July 24, 1975. Naval Historical Center, Washington, D.C.

Index

Page numbers for illustrations are in boldface

About the Author

"After researching and writing books for the *Letters from the Homefront* series, it was fascinating to take a look at America's wars from a different point of view in *Letters from the Battlefront.* While I read the letters, diaries, and reflections of soldiers from the American Revolution all the way through the Vietnam War, I was struck once again by the way, in our fast-changing world, people themselves remain so little changed. The Continental soldier shivering at Valley Forge and the army infantryman in the jungles of South Vietnam wore different uniforms and carried different weapons. They  sometimes used different words to express their feelings. But beneath the skin, their basic concerns and emotions—their love of life, their longing for home and family, their search for meaning amid the bewildering inhumanity of war—were startlingly similar."

VIRGINIA SCHOMP has written more than forty books on nonfiction topics including ancient cultures and American history. Ms. Schomp lives in the Catskill Mountain region of New York with her husband, Richard, and their son, Chip.